Making the Jump

Transition to work

A guide to supporting adults with learning difficulties make the jump from education to employment

niace
promoting adult learning

Yola Jacobsen

Published by the National Institute of Adult Continuing Education
(England and Wales)

21 De Montfort Street
Leicester
LE1 7GE

Company registration no. 2603322
Charity registration no. 1002775

First published 2002

Thanks to Blackburn College and Bolton Community College for permission to use
the images herein.

NIACE, the National Institute of Continuing Adult Education, has a broad remit to
promote lifelong opportunities for adults. NIACE works to develop increased
participation in education and training. It aims to do this for those who do not have
easy access because of class, gender, age, race, language and culture, learning
difficulties or disabilities, or insufficient financial resources.

You can find NIACE online at www.niace.org.uk

Cataloguing in Publication Data
A CIP record of this title is available from the British Library

ISBN   1 86201 143 5

Typeset by Boldface, London
Printed and bound in the UK by Aspect Binders and Print Ltd

Contents

Acknowledgements

NIACE would like to thank the following people and organisations for their invaluable help and support with this project:

The Department of Health, who funded the project research and the development of these materials through a grant from Section 64.

Mencap, for their financial support in the production of *'We can do a good job'*, the learners' pack.

The people and organisations we visited and those who sent information to us.

Andrew Bright, Self-advocate and Consultant.

Greg Everatt, Project Consultant, January–June 2001.

Peter Lavender, NIACE.

Brian McGinnis, Specialist Advisor, Mencap.

Ken Simons, Senior Research Fellow, Norah Fry Research Centre.

Sarah Sodhi, NIACE.

The project steering group for their support and advice:
   Paul Adeline, CHANGE.
   Steve Beyer, Welsh Centre for Learning Disabilities.
   Deborah Cooper (Chair), Milton Keynes Council and member of
      NIACE Executive Committee.
   David Ellis, Department of Health.
   Sally Faraday, Learning and Skills Development Agency.

Margaret Kingsford, Hopwood Hall College.
John Lawton, Mencap, Education Officer.
Lesley Lewis, Bolton Community College.
Liz Maudslay, Skill, the National Bureau for Students with
    Disabilities.
Jeannie Sutcliffe, Development Officer, NIACE.

Special thanks to Liz Maudslay for her help with writing the
publications; Greg Everatt for his work on the project; and Anne
Agius for her secretarial support.

Foreword

It is a pleasure to introduce this important publication from NIACE.

Increasing employment opportunities and seeing employment as a valid option for all people with learning disabilities are central objectives in the Department of Health publication, *Valuing People* (2001). The work that has led to this report has identified good practice examples of vocational courses or training where adults with learning difficulties are making the transition from education to employment. Helping to ensure that people are supported and enabled to make this move is an important challenge in making this vision a reality.

In describing how this has been achieved across the country, this publication draws out key messages for developing effective transition to work provision that can and should be replicated by others.

One important finding of the Making the Jump project is that employment is a realistic goal for the whole range of people with learning difficulties – a fact understood by many people but sadly still challenged by some. This belief, along with organisational factors, such as the importance of the education service in partnership working and the key role of carers in supporting people into work, is identified as a key component of successful transitions from education to employment.

This pack is important for staff working with people with learning difficulties in the education service and beyond. Along with the accessible learners' pack, *'We can do a good job'*, I am sure that *Transition to work* will prove an important tool in helping people make a worthwhile contribution to the world of work.

Rob Greig
Valuing People Director of Implementation

Introduction

'We can do a good job.'

'College helped, it gave me time to think about what to do.'

'Don't get a job straightaway, do a training course first.'

'I want paid employment.'

This pack looks at how adults with learning difficulties can be supported to make the transition from vocational education or training into employment. It is based on the findings of a 2-year project funded by the Department of Health (DoH), Making the Jump – Transition to work.

Throughout the pack, examples of transition to work provision are used to illustrate how people with learning difficulties are being supported to progress onto work, and how successful provision is being developed. Issues for managers and policy makers to address are highlighted in order to focus on ways that transition to work provision can be strengthened to become an integral part of education and training services for adults with learning difficulties.

What was the purpose of the Making the Jump project

Many people with learning difficulties fail to make the jump from attending further or adult education training courses or attending Social Services day services to paid employment. For example only 8 per cent of people with learning difficulties in supported-employment schemes have progressed there from a further education college (Beyer, Goodere and Kilsby, 1996). A familiar story is of individuals remaining at college for years, sometimes repeating courses, or returning to the day centre from which they were originally referred, only to come back to college a few years later.

A recent Scottish study (Riddell, Baron and Wilson, 2001) showed people with learning difficulties caught in a cycle of continual attendance of 'special classes'. They were not meeting new people and developing wider social networks. In this way the classes they attended 'served to bind them into the limited circuit of special provision'. Despite extensive periods of training and education, the individuals involved in the study rarely progressed onto using their skills in wider and more open contexts such as employment. One of the older people involved in the study was '...about to "retire" from the training round, without ever having had the opportunity to put the training into practice'.

The Making the Jump project set out to find examples of good practice of vocational courses or training where adults with learning difficulties are making the transition onto employment.

Why is transition to work important?

'We want to open the door to employment and bring about an inclusive future'.

Malcolm Wicks, former minister for lifelong learning, speaking at the DfES seminar on progression into employment for people with learning difficulties, March 15th 2001.

'I get paid into my bank account. I feel excellent, really happy.'

Work is important to all of us, not only for the money we may earn but also because work provides status, the opportunity to develop skills, the chance to develop self-confidence, make friends and widen our social circle. People with learning difficulties can benefit in these ways as much as, if not more than, the rest of us. For many years people with learning difficulties have tended to spend large proportions of their time either in segregated settings or with people who are paid to be with them. Work offers a way for people with learning difficulties to spend time with ordinary people in ordinary settings and make a positive contribution in their local communities.

Increasing the number of people with learning difficulties in paid work is one of the objectives highlighted in *Valuing People*, the government's White Paper on services for people with learning difficulties. The government recognises that employment for people with learning difficulties is '...*an important route to social inclusion...*' (DoH, 2001).

However, the statistics below give a picture of the extent to which disabled people are excluded from the world of work (Office for National Statistics, Spring 2001):

● Disabled people are seven times more likely to be out of work and on benefits compared to non-disabled people

● The long-term unemployment rate for disabled people is double that of non-disabled people

● Disabled people are twice as likely to have no qualifications as non-disabled people

● It is estimated that less than 10 per cent of people with learning difficulties are in employment.

Surveys of people with disabilities, such as the survey carried out in Bolton for the Welfare to Work Joint Investment Plan, indicate that 60–70 per cent of those who responded would like to be employed in ordinary workplaces. However, anecdotal evidence suggests that people with learning difficulties, on achieving a vocational qualification, are much more likely to move onto further training or a day centre than they are to work.

The *Charter for Learning*, made by and for people with learning difficulties (NIACE, 2000), includes the following as one of the 12 charter points:

'The right to be able to do a course to get a job.'

In the pack that accompanies the charter (Jacobsen, 2000), people with learning difficulties go on to say:

'We want learning to give us the skills to maybe get a job.'

'There should be a chance of work or money at the end of the course.'

'Learning helps you try for a better job. Helps you plan for the future.'

Who is this pack for?

This pack is designed to be a practical resource primarily for staff and managers working with people with learning difficulties in education. However, as multi-agency collaboration is crucial in this area of work, this pack will also be of interest to staff in Social Services, health and voluntary organisations. Parents and carers may find this pack of interest. Businesses and organisations that employ people with learning difficulties could also find parts of the pack a useful reference tool.

A pack for people with learning difficulties, *'We can do a good job'*, accompanies this staff pack. It offers a learner-centred perspective to developing provision and can be used as a resource to complement this pack. *'We can do a good job'* can also be used as a stand-alone pack for people with learning difficulties in self-advocacy organisations or student groups.

How to use the pack

This pack can be used in several different ways. You may only want to refer to specific sections, or it may suit your purpose better to work through the text as a whole. The first chapter presents the main findings of the project. The focus of the following two chapters is on the examples of transition to work provision visited for the project. Key points that emerged from the fieldwork visits are highlighted in these chapters. Chapter 4 discusses planning and funding transition to work provision. An outline of the rules and regulations regarding benefits and their effect on earnings is provided in chapter 5. Chapter 6 looks at the components of a transition to work curriculum. An overview of relevant policy initiatives that should be considered when developing transition to work provision is provided in chapter 7. This chapter also includes some key messages for managers to consider when developing transition to work provision. Each chapter ends with a summary and some questions aimed at drawing out key issues to consider. Chapter 8, the final chapter of the pack, contains an action plan designed to be used as a practical tool by those who want to develop transition to work provision. The appendices provide a list of the fieldwork visits undertaken for the project and a summary of the project findings and recommendations. This is in the form of an information sheet that could be copied and given to relevant senior managers. A list of useful organisations and resources is included at the end of the pack.

This pack could provide:

- Material for staff-development sessions
- A source of ideas and information for those developing new or existing transition to work provision
- A reference source to use when arguing the case for transition to work provision.

The Making the Jump project – ways of working

A few examples of transition to work provision based in education were known to the Making the Jump project at the start. However, to find further examples a call for information was sent out to further and adult education networks, posted on websites and published in relevant journals. The project was looking for examples of courses or training in continuing education that include transition to work as an integral part of the curriculum on offer. Further contact was initiated with a wide range of organisations that might be expected to be involved in this transition process. These included colleges of further education, community-based education and training organisations, specialist supported-employment providers and learning disability advocacy organisations.

Some of these contacts were followed up with visits. The criteria upon which the decision to make visits was based included whether:

- The provision was innovative or at a key stage of development
- The provision had an established track record and was seen to exemplify good practice models
- The provision was seen to be developing existing models.

The fieldwork visits were used as an opportunity to talk to both staff and learners about their experiences of transition to work provision. To keep up-to-date with the plethora of policy initiatives around employment for disabled people and to get an overview of existing research in this area, a literature search was carried out.

Summary

- Previous research indicates that few people with learning difficulties succeed in progressing from vocational courses in continuing education to employment. The Making the Jump – Transition to work project set out to find examples of provision in post-16 education and training where learners are making the transition to work.
- The benefits of employment to people with learning difficulties are no different from the benefits experienced by the rest of us. Work has an added value for people with learning difficulties, as it can be a way of getting out of segregated settings and being included in 'ordinary' life.
- *Valuing People*, the DoH strategy for services for people with learning difficulties for the twenty-first century, recognises employment as an important way to include people with learning difficulties in society.
- Current surveys and studies highlight the extent to which people with learning difficulties are excluded from employment and the importance people with learning difficulties place on having a job.

- The project was looking for examples of transition to work provision in post-16 education that were innovative and good practice. Various colleges, community education services and voluntary organisations were visited.

Checklist

★ Are you aware of the strategy in your area to implement the recommendations of the *Valuing People* report?

★ What are the views of the people with learning difficulties that you work with about employment?

★ Is there any formal transition to work provision from education to employment in your area?

The next chapter looks at the main findings of the Making the Jump project.

References

Beyer S, Goodere L and Kilsby M (1996) *The Costs and Benefits of Supported Employment Agencies*, Department for Education and Employment

DoH (2001) *Valuing People: A new strategy for learning disability for the 21st century*, Department of Health

Jacobsen, Y (ed) (2000) *Our Right to Learn: A pack for people with learning difficulties and staff who work with them, based on the Charter for Learning*, National Institute of Adult Continuing Education

NIACE (2000) *Charter for Learning*, National Institute of Adult Continuing Education

Office for National Statistics (Spring 2001) *Labour Force Survey Quarterly Supplement*, Stationery Office

Riddell S, Baron S and Wilson A (2001) *The Learning Society and People with Learning Difficulties*, The Policy Press

Resources

NIACE has published a number of books and packs on education for adults with learning difficulties.

Macadam M and Sutcliffe J (1996) *Still A Chance to Learn? A report on the impact of the Further and Higher Education Act (1992) on education for adults with learning difficulties*, National Institute of Adult Continuing Education

NIACE/CHANGE (1998) *Training for Change: A training pack to support adults with learning disabilities to become trainers*, National Institute of Adult Continuing Education

Simons K and Sutcliffe J (1993) *Self-Advocacy and Adults with Learning Difficulties: Context and debates*, National Institute of Adult Continuing Education

Sutcliffe J (1996a) *Enabling Learning: A student-centred approach to teaching adults with learning difficulties*, National Institute of Adult Continuing Education

Sutcliffe J (1996b) *Towards Inclusion: Developing integrated education for adults with learning difficulties*, National Institute of Adult Continuing Education

Sutcliffe J (1993) *Integration for Adults with Learning Difficulties: Contexts and debates*, National Institute of Adult Continuing Education

Sutcliffe J (1990) *Adults with Learning Difficulties: Education for choice and empowerment*, NIACE/Open University Press

Sutcliffe J and Jacobsen Y (1998) *All Things Being Equal? A practical guide to widening participation for adults with learning difficulties in education*, National Institute of Adult Continuing Education

Main findings

1

This chapter looks at the main findings of the Making the Jump – transition to work project. Seventeen project fieldwork visits were made to further education colleges, adult and community education services, a volunteer centre, supported employment agencies and voluntary sector organisations run by and for people with learning difficulties (see Appendix 1). Managers, practitioners and people with learning difficulties were interviewed about the provision they were involved in. Information from a number of meetings, conferences and seminars, which focussed on different aspects of employment and disabled people, contributed to the project research, including:

- Greater London Employment Network on Disability, Employment and Training Conference, June 2000
- Disability North Conference, Employment Issues: Disability, February 2001
- 5th European Union of Supported Employment Conference, March 2001
- DfES 'Making Progress': Progression into Employment for Students with Learning Difficulties Seminar, March 2001.

Main findings

Examples of transition to work provision were rare and difficult to find

It was not easy to find transition to work provision for people with learning difficulties based in continuing education. The project received a lot of information about examples of vocational courses in further and adult education, but these courses rarely included a planned programme of transition where a learner continues to receive support even when they have progressed into employment. A couple of well-established examples of transition to work provision were known about at the start of the project. Other examples emerged during the project after some concerted investigation. Several providers were in the early stages of developing transition to work provision. Where good provision does exist the numbers of people with learning difficulties actually achieving employment are still very low. This highlights the urgent need for this area of work to be taken seriously at a national level.

Funding for transition to work provision was fragile

No single funding source covered all aspects of transition to work provision. Pooling resources from several different sources was essential. Usually there was an element of the funding that was short term, in particular ESF (European Social Fund) grants funding the work of supported employment agencies. In some cases, the capacity of the supported employment service was limited due to lack of funding to expand and develop its services. This had a direct effect on how many people could be supported in their transition from education to work.

At the time of the fieldwork visits, two projects were waiting to hear about funding applications to Europe before they could develop the provision further. A couple of other projects were actively fundraising in order to develop their provision. In one case, transition work between a supported employment agency and a college was funded by a 2-year grant from a large utilities firm. The money received was intended to act as pump priming money. The long-term aim was to find an agency to take over running and funding the provision at the conclusion of the initial project. Discussions were held with both the college and Social Services staff but no agreement to carry on the work was reached. Therefore, when the grant ended the provision ceased. The majority of examples of transition to work provision in colleges that featured in a national 1997 report (Hughes and Kingsford, 1997), now no longer exist due to the end of specific funding for the work. The provision, although successful, had not been incorporated into the general programme on offer to people with learning difficulties.

Partnership working is key for transition to work provision

All the examples of transition to work provision involved partnership working between different agencies. A wide range of organisations was involved in delivering the provision. The nature of the partnership varied depending upon how the provision was being delivered. Several types of transition to work provision emerged from the examples studied for the project. A link between education or training and some form of employment service, usually a supported employment agency, was essential for the success of transition to work provision.

Several key factors for successful transition to work provision

Key factors for success include:
- Recognition that employment is a realistic goal for people with learning difficulties
- Training packages to suit the individual learner

- Finding out at the start of the course what area of employment the learner is interested in and what employment opportunities are available locally
- Supported work experience placements
- Organised long-term support for the individual once he or she is in work
- Support for the employer from supported employment agency staff
- Involving parents in the process
- Good working relationships between the different agencies involved in the transition to work provision
- The support of senior managers of relevant services
- Access to specialist advice, e.g. benefits.

Some factors that do not help the development of effective transition to work provision are:

- Long-term work experience with no clear plan for progression to paid employment
- Unsupported work experience placements where an individual could be set up to fail if support is not available
- Courses that are too general and not focussed on the main aim of transition to work.

The effect of earnings on benefits claimed by individuals, is often perceived as a barrier to getting paid work

The effects of earning on benefits that individuals receive are complex and changing.

> *'I can't earn too much because the government takes our money off us.'*

> *'We want our own money for working, real wages not benefits.'*

'I don't want a job basically because I will lose my benefits.'

'I have to make sure that I don't get more money or I will lose my sick benefit.'

Having access to specialist advice and clear information about benefits was key to the success of transition to work provision. In one instance staff felt the process of working out the implications of earnings on benefits to be so difficult that voluntary work was seen to be the safe option. In other cases, staff had incorrect information about how benefits would affect income. As a consequence they were setting relatively low targets for learners in terms of hours worked and wages earned when considering employment options.

Transition to work provision is often the result of ad hoc arrangements

In some areas transition to work provision is being developed as part of an overall strategic plan of services for people with learning difficulties. As such, it has some chance of becoming an established part of the services. Often however, transition to work provision has developed as a result of ad hoc arrangements. One key individual or group may drive the work, but in time this makes the work vulnerable. In such cases staff can work in isolation. Unless the provision is taken on board, as an essential element of the vocational curriculum, it is very vulnerable to changes in staff and circumstances.

Many people with learning difficulties want to have the chance to work

People with learning difficulties said that they value the opportunity to learn skills that will help them get employment.

'The course is really useful to be on.'

'It is important to start as a trainee, you have to work on it and after that you get paid.'

Individuals who were interviewed for the project were very clear that they wanted to work. These are some of the reasons they gave:

'To earn some money.'

'To stop being bored at home.'

'You meet more people.'

'Work gives you the chance to learn new things, more difficult things.'

'It keeps me out of mischief.'

'You can pay the bills.'

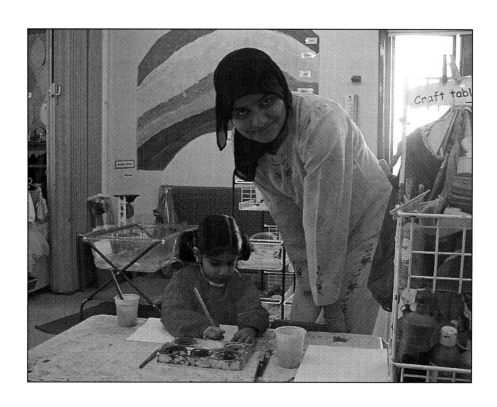

The attitudes of others were a barrier that some people with learning difficulties, who want to work, have had to challenge:

'We don't want people to say we can't work – please give us support if we have problems.'

'Get real – believe in me and help me believe in myself.'

'Give us a chance to show what we can do.'

'Never give up, try and go for something you enjoy. People didn't think I could ever work.'

The learners' pack that accompanies this pack, *'We can do a good job'*, contains further comments and ideas from people with learning difficulties about work and the transition to work.

Summary

- Transition to work provision based in continuing education does exist. However, examples are rare and difficult to find.
- Funding for transition to work provision is fragile, as it is often reliant on time-limited grants. Short-term funding can be valuable if it is used as pump-priming money, however examples of provision funded in this way are vulnerable. If they are not incorporated into the core programme of courses on offer to people with learning difficulties, they tend to disappear when the grants end.
- Partnership working with other agencies is key for transition to work provision. A wide range of organisations can be involved.
- Several key factors for successful transition to work provision can be identified.
- The perceived effect of earnings on benefits, combined with a lack of clear and accurate information about what is possible, can be a major barrier to working for people with learning difficulties.

- Transition to work provision is often driven by key committed individuals. Provision that is developed as an integral part of educational opportunities that are on offer to people with learning difficulties is rare.
- Many people with learning difficulties value the opportunity to train for work and progress onto employment. Work may not be everyone's preferred option but it is important that it should be one of a range of opportunities that people with learning difficulties can choose from.

Checklist

★ What are the current progression routes for learners with learning difficulties on vocational courses where you work?

★ Is there potential to build on existing working relationships with other organisations in your area, to develop transition to work provision?

★ How can the views of people with learning difficulties inform the development of transition to work provision?

The next chapter describes several examples of transition to work provision visited as part of the fieldwork for the Making the Jump project.

References

Hughes M and Kingsford M (1997) *A Real Job – With Prospects: Supported employment opportunities for adults with learning difficulties and disabilities*, FEDA

Transition to work provision in further/ adult and community education

2

This chapter addresses ways that different examples of transition to work provision have developed. The examples in this chapter show further and adult education providers working in partnership with some form of supported employment service.

Supported employment

Supported employment services specialise in working with disabled people to help them find work and to provide ongoing, one-to-one support once they are in employment. Historically, this approach has been used mainly with people with learning difficulties, although people with mental health difficulties and other disabilities can also find this method helpful.

Supported employment agencies are voluntary sector organisations that provide a range of employment services for disabled people. Supported employment services are available in some areas as part of the employment services of Social Services Departments. The Making the Jump project found supported employment in both of these forms, working in partnership with colleges and LEAs (Local Education Authorities) to deliver transition to work provision for people with learning difficulties.

In supported employment the focus is usually on finding 'real jobs in the community' rather than sheltered employment. One of the principles of supported employment is a strong belief that no one who wants to work is unemployable. Supported employment develops individualised support packages with and for the person they are helping.

Supported employment

Supported employment agencies will typically be able to offer a combination of:

- **Vocational profiles** to help people identify the individual's skills and preferences
- **Job development** to find the person's preferred job through contact with employers
- **Job analysis** to find out more about the workplace, co-workers and the support an individual might need in that environment
- **Job support** to ensure that both the employee and employer receive 'just enough' creative assistance, information and back-up to achieve success – with this support continuing as long as it is needed
- **Career support** to help people think in the longer term about career progression.

(O'Bryan, Simons, Beyer, 2001)

Transition to work provision

This section describes some of the examples of transition to work provision that were part of the project fieldwork. Whilst the examples are quite distinct from each other in many ways, sometimes common themes emerged around how provision originated and was organised. Three main kinds of provision are described:

- Changing Days
- Further education and supported employment
- Adult/community education and supported employment.

Changing Days

Changing Days is the name of a 1996 report from the King's Fund Centre. The report was based on a project looking at how day opportunities for people with learning difficulties could be developed. One of the key principles of the project was that:

> *'the future for people with learning disabilities should be away from segregated day centres and buildings-based services towards people with learning disabilities being given support to participate in ordinary activities in the community.'* (Wertheimer 1996)

Supported employment was highlighted by the report as being a key part of developing new daytime opportunities for people with learning difficulties.

The work of the Changing Days project has been influential on the reorganisation of day services for people with learning difficulties. It has encouraged the development of services away from building-based provision, such as day centres, to activities based in ordinary community-based settings. Croydon and Buckinghamshire have established transition to work provision as a result of a wider review and reorganisation of day services for people with learning difficulties in their area. They exemplify the approach advocated in *Changing Days*.

Croydon

In Croydon, the reorganisation of day services coincided with the end of a 2-year ESF (European Social Fund) Connections project involving education, Social Services and STATUS Employment; a well-established, local, supported employment agency. The ESF project came about as organisations, working with people with learning difficulties in Croydon, recognised the need to work together more closely in order to provide coherent services that supported individuals to progress. The aim of the project was to support adults with learning difficulties in the development of skills to become more independent. Work experience and supported employment opportunities had been one aspect of the project. When the ESF funding for the Connections project ended the project was incorporated into the reorganised resource-based model of day services. The strategic partnership between the different agencies was maintained and the reorganised day services kept the name of the original ESF project, Connections.

Three of the former ESF projects' posts are now funded by Social Services and based in a resource centre (formerly a day centre): the Connections Project Manager, a Voluntary Placements Co-ordinator and a Work Experience Co-ordinator. A Supported Employment Worker post, to arrange supported employment opportunities, although funded by Social Services, is based in the offices of STATUS Employment. The borough's Community Education Service, Croydon Continuing Education and Training Service (CETS), has taken on a part-time Guidance Worker post from the project.

The Learning for Work course is a 30-week course for adults with learning difficulties. The Head of Learning Support at CETS described the course as being for learners *'interested in developing their skills for work and independent living'*. The course was funded by the Further Education Funding Council (FEFC) and was based at the main CETS adult education centre. People interested in the course are referred from the Social Services day centre and group homes in the area. The Connections Work Experience Co-ordinator teaches on the course, preparing people for work experience and organising work placements. The local authority Social Services Department funds her work on the course. Learners can progress onto supported employment opportunities arranged by the Social Services Department-funded worker based at STATUS Supported Employment Agency.

Buckinghamshire

In Buckinghamshire a countywide review of day centres for adults with learning difficulties led to the development of a service with more college and work options. In the south of the county, the restructure of services led to the creation of three new full-time Education Liaison Officer (ELO) posts based at Amersham and Wycombe College. The ELO posts were initially a 1-year secondment to the college from three Social Services resource centres for people with learning difficulties. The role of the ELOs was to ease the transfer of people from the resource centres to the college. This included setting up individuals' programmes and providing support so there was a smooth move to services delivered in an educational setting. After 16 months the ELO posts were made permanent and became part of the college staff team.

Amersham and Wycome College works in partnership with Buckinghamshire Agency for Supported Employment (BASE). BASE is part funded by the ESF and the local authority and is based in Buckinghamshire Social Services Department. BASE offers a supported employment service that covers the whole of Buckinghamshire county and specialises in assisting disabled people to access training, education and paid employment. People with learning difficulties make up the main cohort of BASE's clients. The Manager of BASE described the organisation as:

> '... customer-led, responding to what people need, not what is available.'

She went on to say that in her experience 'customers' want two things in life: a job and a relationship:

> 'This is no different from anyone else, that's what it is all about.'

College and BASE staff work closely together. BASE's Supported Employment Officers refer people with learning difficulties who want to train for work to the college. The ELOs carry out a college assessment to find out what the learners want to do and what skills they already have for work. The purpose of the assessment is to make sure that learners' training programmes meet the needs identified by BASE. For example, it may be that an individual, already on work experience set up by BASE, requires help recognising key words in the workplace or support with money skills. Alternatively an assessment for an individual who wants to work could lead onto them starting college taster courses with a view to vocational choices leading onto work experience. As one ELO explained:

'We work out, with Supported Employment Officers, training packages for people that look at the whole of the working week. BASE assesses what the student needs and we transfer it into a learning programme. Education Liaison Officers and Supported Employment Officers work as a team. There is an important relationship between training and work. You can get immediate feedback on how someone is doing with one link made with the workplace.'

BASE uses information from a County Council database that details the daytime weekly timetables of individuals with learning difficulties who are using a variety of different services. They find this very helpful when working with individuals planning their work experience. BASE will try and fix work experience for individuals that does not clash with their college days. The data also provides information about an individual's past courses, placements and work.

Talkback Self Advocacy

Another key partner is the independent self-advocacy organisation, Talkback Self Advocacy. Talkback run regular meetings at the day centres and they work with people going into college. A woman with learning difficulties who works at Talkback pointed out that staff relationships have a very strong influence on what happens in the lives of people with learning difficulties. Therefore, a group run by an independent organisation can offer more space for people to make their own choices and speak up.

Issues that come up in the self-advocacy groups are fed back to BASE and the college. For instance, someone might want:
- To work more days
- To change their job
- To be more independent in work and reduce their support.

In one case there were problems with a course and people were dropping out. The college asked Talkback to discuss the course with the learners. In the discussions with Talkback, people can talk about what they think is good or bad and what they want to change about college.

As more people at the college and day centres are actually being supported into work, this has a knock-on effect on the aspirations of other people. As one of the Talkback workers explained:

> 'Hearing people talk about their work has a positive effect on others.'

Points to consider

The transition to work provision in Croydon and Buckinghamshire share several characteristics:

- Both have their backgrounds in the reorganisation of day services for people with learning difficulties
- There is a commitment to transition to work at a high level in the different partnership organisations with the involvement of senior managers in the reorganisation of day services
- Employment is recognised as being a realistic and valuable option for people with learning difficulties
- Joint working between education and supported employment has been accepted as being key to transition to work provision for people with learning difficulties
- Resources from the different services have been dedicated to transition to work provision
- As the wider day services for people with learning difficulties evolve, transition to work provision will be an integral part of the services.

This way of developing and delivering transition provision can provide challenges:

- In one instance, day centre staff were resistant to the new focus of a reorganised day service on college and work opportunities. They were brought into college to see what was happening for the learners and involved in joint-training with colleagues in another part of the county who were already working effectively with college and supported employment staff.

- As with any close partnership, it is only as strong as the component parts. If one organisation has funding difficulties then the whole provision could be weakened. Staff cited the reapplication for ESF funding to continue the work of supported employment organisations as a particular concern.

- Staff emphasised the importance of working closely with parents and carers, as their support is crucial. They need to be consulted and involved in the process of changing services as it will have a real impact on their lives.

Further education and supported employment

The common feature of the following examples of transition to work provision is that the joint working is between further education and supported employment services or agencies.

Accrington and Rossendale College

At the time of the project fieldwork visit, Accrington and Rossendale were in the early stages of developing transition to work provision in partnership with Jigsaw Supported Employment. Jigsaw Supported Employment is a voluntary organisation based in Clitheroe, Lancashire.

Accrington and Rossendale College had contracted Jigsaw to find employment for three people with learning difficulties. Jigsaw had responsibility for travel training and contacting and negotiating with employers. Staff from Jigsaw came into college to meet the learners, carry out vocational profiles and, when necessary, find work placements and support the individuals in them.

Although at the time of the visit, the partnership had only placed three people in employment, the experience of one of these learners demonstrates the power of this way of working.

Case study

Jean had been attending various building courses for some time, clearly not enjoying them in spite of her often repeating that she wanted to do building. It was only after a member of staff from Jigsaw Supported Employment was able to make a home visit that it was discovered that Jean was a passionate model maker, which she described as 'building'. This information was fed back to the college.

Jean found work at a double-glazing manufacturer making cut outs and other models for the sales team to use on their visits. She stopped doing the building course at college and started a course that enables her to develop skills in the use of small tools.

Warrington Collegiate Institute

Warrington Collegiate Institute is a large further education college. The college had been running vocational courses for people with learning difficulties for some time but were becoming increasingly aware that there was a need to develop a structured transition from college to whatever the individual chooses to do next.

It was identified that there was a need to support those learners wishing to make a transition from college to open employment. A meeting between key individuals from Warrington Borough Council Social Services and Warrington Collegiate Institute took place. A proposal was made to form a partnership, initially for a 12-month period, and the Access to Community and Employment project (ACE) was established. At the time of writing this pack the project was in its second year.

Warrington Borough Council granted the ACE project development funding that was used to provide job coaches. Existing learning support staff were provided with additional job coach training where they learnt about how to support individuals at work. The training was jointly delivered by a senior member of staff from the college's supported learning section and a Work Placement Officer from Warrington Borough Council's Supported Employment Service. In addition, the Council's Supported Employment Service was partnered with the ACE project to provide expertise in the job finding and employer liaison aspects of the project.

At the time of the project visit, the ACE project was in its first year. Eight people had been accepted onto the course, this number was expected to grow in the following year. The Supported Employment Service, with whom the ACE project is a partner, is a well-established Social Services provider. There are two Work Placement Officers with some limited additional support capacity. By being partnered with the ACE project, and therefore having access to the job coach resource, they were able to place seven learners in work experience placements very quickly. The link with the college is recognised to be a useful selling point when contacting employers.

The college uses Individual Learning Plans (ILPs) and links them to the ASDAN Workright package. College training is tailored to the ILP, which has itself been tailored to the needs and aspirations of the individual. Other than specialist training input, all ACE project activity takes place away from the college campus at an outreach centre. This is seen as a progressive move away from college life, a next step towards the world of work and gaining more independence. People on the course are expected to be either independent travellers or if not, they will be supported with travel training plans to learn to travel independently.

The early stage of the course includes a variety of introductory programs and job tasters. During this time the employment service staff are able to meet and become familiar with the individual's aspirations (they are based in the same building) prior to undertaking a job search. At this stage implications for benefits are explored and decisions made as to the numbers of hours and rates of pay.

Blackburn College

Each year at Blackburn College approximately 80 people with learning difficulties attend courses with a vocational component, with a view to getting a job. These learners will typically spend 4 years at college. There are about 20 people graduating each year who need support in finding or keeping employment.

All the courses at Blackburn College are mainstream courses. Specialist tutors are employed strategically in departments that can typically be expected to attract large numbers of applications from people with learning difficulties. In addition some tutors are assigned extra time per learner in order to accommodate their particular learning needs and a body of classroom support staff is available.

The type of courses that are often offered to people with learning difficulties, such as independent living skills, are not offered at Blackburn College, as the content of these courses are integrated with the mainstream courses. For example, personal presentation and communication skills are incorporated into the reception element of Hairdressing and Beauty. It is in this way that the college believes it can best serve its learners, equipping them with not only the vocational skills required but also the social skills necessary to enhance early and effective integration into the workforce.

Most people with learning difficulties are engaged in accredited training, typically National Vocational Qualifications (NVQs). However, these courses are not considered appropriate for a small number of learners, and for these ILPs are produced. The structure most frequently used as a basis for the ILPs is the ASDAN Workright course. The ASDAN documentation has been useful as a focus for tutors. A lot of the ASDAN resources have been adapted to make them specific to the individual learner's work placements.

The Workwise course has been part of the provision at Blackburn College for 5 years. The course is for people with learning difficulties who do not slot into other courses because of what they want to do and the support they need. Work experience placements are part of the Workwise course.

Case study

Meera is a young woman on the Workwise course, who is on work placement at a play group. Meera has personal tutorials to assess and review her progress and support needs. She does individualised portfolio work with a tutor for *'things she needs to know for her work placement'*. This fits in with the ASDAN Workright accreditation. Support with the practical aspect of organising activities with young children is part of the Foundation Play certificate. Meera attends small group sessions for basic skills in Maths, English and Computers.

Case study

Philip had not worked for many years. He met with the Workwise course tutor to talk about the type of work placement he would like to do and other skills he would like to try and find out more about. He wanted to try a work placement at a car garage to find out more about car mechanics and to improve his reading and filling-in of job sheets and forms.

This is what Philip did during the week:

Monday afternoon – work placement at local garage.

Tuesday morning – meeting with tutor and five other people. Spends time reading and writing job sheets, order forms and invoices. Also uses the computer.

Wednesday morning – meets with the course tutor to talk about the work and to keep information in a file. Go for a coffee and have a chat about the week to check if everything is going okay.

Thursday afternoon – back at the garage.

When they have completed the Workwise course, individuals who would benefit from continued support once in employment are referred to the Supported Employment Service of the Social Services Department for Blackburn and Darwen.

Between 1997 and 2001, 27 learners completed the Workwise course. They went on to do a variety of different things, shown in the table below.

Employment	8
Referred to supported employment agencies	4
Voluntary work	2
Took the Work Wise course for a second year	3
Other courses	5
Decided against pursuing employment	2
Put employment 'on hold'	1
Referred on to a specialist outreach service	1
Moved out of the area at the end of the course	1

Mencap Pathway Employment Service and Harrow College

Mencap Pathway Employment Service in Harrow was established in 1998 to support people with learning difficulties into work. The Pathway Service has a specific link to Harrow College, with its office situated in the main college building. It is supported by the ESF and Harrow College provides matched funding for the partnership in the form of premises costs and an administrative post. Two full-time workers staff the Pathway Service.

Mencap Pathway Employment Services provide employment services for people with learning difficulties. Individuals are supported by the service through training for work; liasion with employers; organising and supporting work experience placements; providing job club facilities; support at interview; benefits advice; finding work; and on-the-job support, as appropriate.

Learners on the ASDAN-certified Foundation Training Award course at Harrow College meet with the Pathway workers in September at the start of their 1-year college course. Together they work on an initial assessment and work profiling. The Pathway workers organise work experience placements for the learners on the course and support them whilst they are on the placements.

They are in a good position to be able to feed back directly to the course tutor about the learners' progress and to highlight any particular area where a learner may need further support. In June, at the end of the course, the learners can chose to become Pathway clients and they are then supported into work, paid or voluntary, or onto further vocational courses. The Pathway workers can offer a continuity of support to individuals, from the course onto the Pathway Employment Service and then in the progression to employment.

The table below shows what the Foundation Training Award course learners, who have progressed on to the Pathway Employment Service, went on to do.

Made the transition to paid employment	7
Gone onto further vocational training	11
Voluntary work	5
ESOL classes	2
Did not take up offers of paid work	3

In some cases, where individuals did not take up the offer of paid employment, it was because their parents felt that the job was:
- Too far away
- Too much of a time commitment and did not fit in to an established routine
- A threat to benefits, especially if their son or daughter received housing benefit.

The Pathway workers identified the support of parents and carers as crucial for individuals to make the transition to work. They felt that it was important that learners and their families know at the start of the college course that the eventual aim is for paid work.

Collaboration between teaching staff and Pathway workers means that the college has adapted aspects of the course to better suit the transition process. For example, it was decided that Pathway's training about job searching should be part of the college course. This close liaison and sharing of experiences also ensures that individual learner's needs are met more effectively. Discussion between Pathway and college staff about issues for particular learners, for instance the need for confidence building, has led to more specific pieces of work being done with them as part of their course.

Points to consider

There are some common characteristics that the transition to work provision at Accrington and Rossendale, Warrington, Blackburn and Harrow share between them:

- The principle partnership for the transition to work provision is between the college and a supported employment agency or service
- In each case the expertise of the supported employment agency is brought in at different stages of the college course
- Three of the colleges use ASDAN accreditation for their courses
- Two of the colleges were in the early stages of developing their transition to work provision
- One college's transition provision was well established; two others had been running for 3 years.

Challenges

- New transition to work provision may need a chance to establish itself so it can then become a part of the core curriculum on offer to people with learning difficulties.
- Working relationships between the partner organisations involved will need time to develop.
- Supported employment agency staff stated that the earlier they were involved in the transition process in partnership with the

colleges, the more effective they could be when supporting people to find employment.

Adult/community education and supported employment

Bolton Community Education Service

A number of years ago Bolton was a pilot area for the resettlement of residents from long-stay hospitals. This led to the need for extensive joint agency working. During the following period there was only a gradual change over of key staff in these agencies allowing this culture of co-operation to be sustained. Strong and positive working relationships have evolved between the partner organisations.

The Borough Council has a clear commitment at both the political and officer level to the inclusion of people with learning difficulties in all aspects of community life. Disabled people, including people with learning difficulties, have been supported in their transition from education to work for a number of years.

Transition to work

In April 2001, Bolton Community Education Service and Bolton College merged to form Bolton Community College. The project visit to Bolton took place just before this merger when Bolton Community Education Service (CES) was a community-based adult education service independent of the college. Bolton CES provided a range of courses aimed specifically at people with learning difficulties and all mainstream courses have two places reserved for people with learning difficulties. Forty-two people with learning difficulties were engaged in training with a specific vocational content. Some of the courses offered generalised work preparation, covering subjects such as health and safety, job skills, self-help and independence, new technology and the arrangement of work experience placements. Other courses provided more specific training in vocational skills in the fields of catering, business administration and retail. Bolton CES offered learners a range of educational options, both leading to accredited qualifications and based upon ILPs, that result in highly individual packages of training being created to suit the requirements of each learner.

Bolton CES works with a partner organisation, Bolton Employment Support Team (BEST). BEST is a partnership between Mencap and Bolton Social Services and is mainly funded by Social Services. All work experience placements and negotiations are managed by BEST. BEST also arranges supported placements and paid employment opportunities with mainstream employers.

BEST works with a range of other organisations in order to provide support, not only education and Social Services but also the Benefits Agency, where they have a named person to whom they can turn for advice, and the Employment Service. Bolton is a pilot area for New Deal Personal Advisors and they have been able to access additional resources through this avenue.

In Bolton there is a range of sheltered work provision. BEST receives referrals from these to support people to move onto supported open employment with local employers. Sheltered work is recognised as having some value for the people involved, particularly if it is incorporated into a progressive sequence. However, it is not the preferred option for the majority of the people with learning difficulties who want to work in open employment.

Points to consider

The strength of the partnership working stood out during the project fieldwork visit to Bolton:
- All the major organisational players wholeheartedly support the achievement of employment outcomes
- They were able to work alongside each other without any of the

inter-organisational arguments that can so often bedevil partnership working

- All the organisations in the partnerships were in agreement about the principles that underpinned their joint working
- The Welfare to Work Joint Investment Plan (JIP – see chapter 7) was well advanced at the time of the visit, involving an impressive degree of community consultation
- The views of all people with a disability appear to be central to the development of Bolton JIP and it is categorically in favour of employment in ordinary settings.

Challenges

- A major issue at Bolton was transport. Although there is a good network of public transport it is inaccessible to many people with learning difficulties due to its complexity. This need not be a problem for people once in work as Access to Work (a government scheme that provides support for disabled people to cover the extra costs of employment) can help fund individual transport needs. However, the process of getting to training and training placements ties up considerable resources either in terms of staff time for travel training or in the provision of taxis or minibuses.
- Benefits were seen as a major barrier to employment. Some learners, and their parents and carers, were loathed to go for full-time employment (over 16-hours a week), because of the possible effect on their benefits. As one member of staff from Bolton CES commented, '*this can mean that students lack confidence to go for it*'.
- At the time of the visit in early 2001, Bolton CES was preparing for a merger with Bolton College. Staff felt that this change would undoubtedly bring benefits in that there will be a much wider range of training resources accessible to learners. However, there was also a fear that the person-centred

approach could be harder to maintain in a very much larger organisation.

Summary

- Further and adult/community education, working in partnership with supported employment services, is the basis of the examples of transition to work provision in this chapter.
- Supported employment can come in the form of agencies that are voluntary sector organisations and services, usually part of Social Services Departments' employment services.
- Supported employment practice focuses on one-to-one support for individuals – working with the individual to look at what they really want to do, the training they need to do this and the support they need when they are on work experience placements and once they are in paid employment. Support for the employer is also crucial.
- Transition to work provision in Buckinghamshire and Croydon has developed as part of a reorganisation of day services for people with learning difficulties.
- Talkback Self Advocacy offer support and encouragement for people with learning difficulties who want to work. This one of a few examples of peer support where people with learning difficulties are supporting each other.
- Further education colleges, when working with supported employment services, can be effective in helping people with learning difficulties in the transition to employment. The provision, whilst being distinctive in each case, does share some common characteristics for success.
- The transition to work provision at Bolton CES was effective because it was based on well-established partnership arrangements between various agencies.

Checklist

★ Which of the types of transition to work provision described in this chapter offers ideas for developing transition to work provision in your particular organisation?

★ What links do you have with supported employment organisations or services in your area and how could they be developed?

★ How can people with learning difficulties be involved in supporting each other in the transition to employment?

The next chapter looks at further examples of transition to work provision.

References

O'Bryan A, Simons K, Beyer S, *et al.* (2001) *A Framework for Supported Employment*, Joseph Rowntree Foundation

Wertheimer A (1996) *Changing Days: Developing new day opportunities with people who have learning difficulties*, King's Fund Publishing

Transition to work provision – different ways of working

3

This chapter looks at some further examples of transition to work provision that were part of the Making the Jump project fieldwork. In the first example a college staff team developed and delivered a complete transition to work package right through to supporting learners to 'make the jump' to paid employment. This is followed by two examples of government-funded transition to work provision delivered in colleges. Next, there are details of how a supported employment agency led a 2-year transition to work initiative that placed people with learning difficulties in paid work. The final example is of a Volunteer Centre working in partnership with a college and a community education provider to find voluntary work opportunities for people with learning difficulties.

Joseph Priestley College

At Joseph Priestley College in Leeds, the development of employment-related skills is seen as an essential element in many of the courses for people with learning difficulties. However, transition to work provision is just starting to develop in the form of the Access to Community and Employment course (ACE). This is a new course and the first intake was in September 2000.

The aim of this 1-year course is to move people into employment where they will work over 16-hours a week, earning at or above the National Minimum Wage. In the first year there was an intake of ten people and it was predicted that six or seven learners would go onto employment. Those that did not would be automatically entitled to re-enter the course and to carry on doing so until they achieved their employment goals, or decided not to.

To join the course applicants have to be committed to seeking full-time work and to be able to travel independently. The travel requirement can be overlooked if there is a reasonable expectation that Access to Work would take on responsibility for payment of a taxi to and from work once the ultimate goal of employment has been achieved. While it is quite reasonable to expect individuals to have progressed through a range of other courses prior to ACE, it is not a requirement. One of the learners on the course had been very clear about his vocational ambitions and had joined the ACE course directly.

Employers are paid a subsidy for work experience placements for individuals on the course. The payment is a way of reinforcing a sense of commitment by the employer to the learner. When these placements are being negotiated, the employer gives an explicit commitment to employ the individual in the long term; this makes these placements more difficult to find, and generally takes longer to negotiate. Identifying a source for the payment to employers has proved a challenge and the college has agreed to make the payment from college funds. It is also planning to hold a fundraising conference to offset the payment.

During the fieldwork visit the project researcher visited five learners in four placements. The placements all varied in the scale and nature of the business – from a five star hotel to a fish and chip restaurant. The most established of these had been running for 8 weeks, others were in their first week. In every case the researcher had the impression that the employers were fully aware of their commitments and their responsibilities, as were the learners.

All the learners were committed to achieving their goal of employment – in spite of an apparent lack of support from family and carers in some cases. Other carers however were both able and willing to provide support when necessary.

Once a learner has made the transition to employment the responsibility for continued support to both employee and employer is handed over to a partner agency that continues until such time as the job comes to a conclusion. At the time of the project visit the college was negotiating with a housing association to provide this long-term support.

Case study

A hotel in Leeds provided a work experience placement for one of the people on the ACE course. This same hotel was a venue for a conference held in the summer term, about the college's transition to employment provision. This was a good opportunity to celebrate and publicise the success of the transition to work provision. On the day of the conference an announcement was made that the learner would be offered a permanent job at the hotel at the end of the course.

There are more details about the curriculum of the ACE course in chapter 6 of this pack.

Points to consider

As with other examples of transition to work provision in further education, the ACE course at Joseph Priestley College supports learners through a vocational course and work placements in preparation for the transition to paid employment. Where this provision differs from others is that:

- The ACE course is organised in such a way that the learner is working towards making the transition into a specific, identified job, right from the beginning of the course
- It is the college staff who find the final job that the learner will make the transition to

- It is when the individual already has secured employment that the college hands over to another agency to provide support for the individual in work.

Challenges

- The driving force behind this provision is the course tutor who had run similar courses before at another college. Provision that is very reliant on individuals is vulnerable if they then move on.
- Money for the subsidy paid to employers had to be fundraised by the college.

Bournemouth and Poole College

Bournemouth and Poole College has a range of courses on offer to people with learning difficulties that have a vocational focus. The aim of the Work Preparation Programme course is to support individuals with various different kinds of disabilities, including learning difficulties, to make the transition to work.

The Work Preparation Programme is run under contract to Employment Services. People are referred to the course from the local Disability Services Team, having had an assessment with the Disability Employment Advisor. The programme has four modules:

- One-to-one guidance and advice
- Personal development course
- Job search skills course
- Work experience placements and job coaches.

At the time of the fieldwork visit there were 45 people with learning difficulties and disabilities using the programme. The programme is time-limited: the typical pattern for learners might involve 4 weeks of personal development and 3 weeks of job search skills, followed by a 6-week (or two 3-week) work placements.

The Work Preparation Programme has a high success rate.

Between 60 and 100 per cent of people completing the programme go onto get paid employment. To count as an employment outcome, the individual would have to be working at least 8 hours in any 7-day period.

Points to consider

- The Work Preparation Programme at Bournemouth and Poole college was the only example of a college, contracted by government employment services to run transition to work provision, brought to the attention of the Making the Jump project.
- The programme is for people with learning difficulties or disabilities.
- Referrals to the Work Preparation Programme come through the Disability Employment Advisor, who has his or her own criteria for who is eligible for the course.

Croydon College and Status Employment Agency

The previous chapter gave details of work in Croydon between STATUS Employment Agency and Croydon Education and Training Services (CETS). This section looks at a transition to work partnership between STATUS and the local further education provider, Croydon College.

The Access to a Working Life programme was a 10-week transitional course run at Croydon College in partnership with STATUS. The programme was funded as a pilot project by the New Deal for Disabled People (NDDP) (see chapter 7). The focus of the New Deal work was on changing the culture around people with learning difficulties and employment. An important way of bringing about this change was to raise the expectations of parents, teachers and key workers by working with them to support people with learning difficulties from the transition from school and college to employment.

Access to a Working Life ran for 2 terms and each term five people with learning difficulties attended the programme for 2 days a week. The programme used the *Status at Work* (Croydon Education Business Partnership, 1996) pack as a basis for its curriculum. This pack was developed in Croydon for use in schools with people with learning difficulties and is intended to introduce young people to issues around employment (further information about the pack is included chapter 6). The ASDAN Workright package was incorporated into the programme to provide accreditation.

The aim of the programme was for people who had completed the course to go onto the STATUS Supported Employment Programme to find paid work. A manager at STATUS recognised that people with learning difficulties at college typically '*... fail to make the transition from full-time education to employment without advocacy support*'.

During the course Employment Consultants from STATUS came into the college and worked with learners. Vocational profiling was integrated within the course and this resulted in the development of individual action plans for each learner. Learners went on three different 'job samples' during the course. Individuals on the programme visited people with learning difficulties, placed in employment by STATUS, at their workplace. The visit was an opportunity for them to spend some time working alongside the worker, who could offer a kind of 'peer support' by talking to the learner about their job and experiences of work.

A STATUS Employment Consultant gave all learners on the programme one-to-one support for all their work experience placements. The placements included:

- Working as an usher in a cinema
- Shelf-stocking in a supermarket
- Working as a porter in a local hospital
- Housekeeping work at a hotel.

Students on the GNVQ Advanced Health and Social Care course worked alongside the Access to a Working Life students as a form of mentoring. The GNVQ learners were involved in an induction with STATUS Employment Consultants to introduce them to the role of the Employment Consultants and the processes and materials used in their work. The inclusion of these learners in the pilot was an attempt to *'influence the professionals of the future'*. The learners on the GNVQ course acted as partners with the learners on the programme and worked alongside them in the classroom. *'They were seen as two students working together.'* They went with them to their job sample visits and helped them set their aims and objectives for the course.

College tutors also worked with STATUS Employment Consultants. They shadowed them in their jobs and visited different sites with them.

Points to consider

- As a pilot for the NDDP the Access to a Working Life programme highlighted the issue of transition to work from education for people with learning difficulties on a national scale.
- This was a short-term course that made use of specific short-term government funding for the NDDP pilot.
- The pre-designed curriculum of the Status at Work pack addressed the specific issues of transition to work from education.
- The involvement of college tutors and GNVQ course members on the Access to a Working Life programme raised awareness of issues concerning people with learning difficulties.

- The 'peer support' offered to individuals on their job sample gave students a valuable context in which to share their experiences.

Challenges

- STATUS and Croydon College recognise the importance of transition work but need to secure further funding in order to develop it.

Independent Neighbourhood Care Association (Inca)

Inca is a small, parent-led, voluntary organisation based in Swinton, Manchester. Inca provides a residential and a supported employment service for people with learning difficulties. About 3 years ago Inca recognised that there was no structured process by which people with learning difficulties at local colleges could move onto either employment or any other daytime activity. They were also aware of a number of individuals who had been placed in unpaid work placements some years earlier and who had continued in these placements, unpaid, without active support from the college or any other agency.

Inca was successful in a bid to British Gas and was able to employ a half-time support worker. The worker's remit was to work with learners at the college who were in the final stages of their education and support them into employment. Inca worked with a local college and was able to recruit a support worker who had earlier worked at the college and was therefore known and trusted by the college.

The worker made presentations to the learners, was invited to join reviews and encouraged college staff to make referrals. However, they were located outside the college with the Inca team.

This was a deliberate policy in order to underline the point that progression from college to employment is not an extension of the college service but a transition to another phase of the person's life.

Over the course of this project eight people were placed into employment. Some of them were placed directly into paid employment, whilst others undertook unpaid work for a period – this was converted into paid work within a short time. At the conclusion of the project none of them required intensive support so Inca were able to absorb them onto their caseload in spite of the fact they did not have a funding package.

The funding for the project was for a 2-year period only. Unfortunately at the end of this time there were no opportunities for this work to be taken on as a core part of college provision for people with learning difficulties and this provision does not exist now. Although this pilot was operated with one local college, Inca has tried to pursue this idea and develop the model with other colleges in the area, though without any success. Its feeling is that colleges do not want to commit resources to buy in services from outside agencies.

Points to consider

The transition provision developed by Inca was clearly effective in placing people in work:

- As a model it can be introduced by one agency with resources, needing a minimum of commitment to the partnership by colleges or other training bodies
- The provision was vulnerable to changes of policy that cut off funding.

Challenges

- A crucial part of the strategy to maintain this work is to find follow-on funding once the initial funding ceases.
- Whilst this particular partnership worked in the short term, if the transition to work provision was to develop it would need a stronger commitment from all partners involved and a source of funding.

Loughborough Volunteer Centre

Loughborough Volunteer Centre has been actively involved for a number of years in enabling people with learning difficulties to take up community activities including voluntary work. The centre liases with two local colleges and a Social Services day centre. The Manager of Loughborough Volunteer Centre, explained:

'Volunteering is actually the single most common route out of the day centre into the community. It is an obvious step for many individuals seeking to progress to employment. It offers experience, new skills, training, social contact, confidence, a reference… the list goes on. Some voluntary placements can actually develop into paid positions.'

Case study

Peter had been involved as a volunteer in a gardening project for several years. As a result of his increased confidence, skills and sense of community belonging he no longer attended a day centre. This left him with a day a week with no planned activities. He began volunteering, using his new skills as a gardener at the community centre where the Volunteer Centre is based. This voluntary activity was so successful that he agreed to become a paid member of staff for a small number of hours each month. A member of the rehabilitation team at Social Services helped to negotiate the slight change in his financial situation with the Benefits Agency and other relevant organisations. Peter explained:

'I do volunteering because the gardens need doing. If I didn't I would be at home watching telly. Now I don't go to the day centre anymore because I've moved on. I've got a job now that I get paid for – doing the gardens.'

At the time of the visit for the Making the Jump project people with learning difficulties were involved in a range of voluntary work opportunities including:

- Catering
- Office/admin work
- Working with older people
- Working with children
- Working at a steam railway trust
- Working at an animal sanctuary
- Gardening.

One person with learning difficulties, involved in voluntary work in an office, commented:

> 'Voluntary work in the office is good experience for me. It will help me to deal with the public, get confidence and get a job in the future. It helps to use the things I learnt in college.'

The Volunteer Centre, in partnership with Rawlings Community College near Loughborough, offers several Open College Network (OCN) accredited programmes for people with learning difficulties in volunteering, self-development and community awareness. All of these programmes are linked closely with voluntary work opportunities and activities.

The Opportunities in Volunteering course is advertised through the local college, Mencap and the Social Services learning difficulties team. The course is not college-based but runs from the Volunteer Centre and is available from Entry Level to Level 3. Learners have to be actively involved in voluntary work for a total of 20 hours. This is arranged by their tutor who offers one-to-one support and tuition for the learner to follow the course. Individuals can take as long as they need to complete the course. Sessions on the course include:

- Choices in voluntary work
- Saying no, getting it wrong and asking for help
- Listening to others' views
- You and others (volunteers and workers)
- Responsibilities as a volunteer
- Responsibilities outside of volunteering (friends, family, etc.).

Staff at the Volunteer Centre were concerned about actual support available once the education system ceases to have a responsibility for an individual involved in volunteering. At the time of the project visit they were submitting a funding application for one worker and two community service volunteers to form a project to offer this support. The project aim was to offer a *'substantial level of support to young people wishing to access volunteering, leisure activities, further education or training and employment'.*

Points to consider

The benefits of involvement in voluntary work are very similar to paid employment:

- The focus of the work between the Volunteer Centre, colleges and day centre is supporting people with learning difficulties to have access to the community
- Voluntary work is seen as a way for people to be involved in the community
- Transition from education to voluntary work can be an end in itself, however in some cases it can prepare people to progress onto paid employment.

Challenges

- To develop this work the Volunteer Centre must seek funding.

Summary

- Several different kinds of partnership support transition to work provision.
- The course at Joseph Priestley College is unusual. It is the college that provides support for the transition from college to employment, including finding the jobs for the people on the course.
- Bournemouth and Poole College has a contract with the government Employment Service to run transition to work provision.

- STATUS and Croydon College ran a course funded as part of the New Deal for Disabled People pilot programme. The short course supported people with learning difficulties into a supported employment programme with a view to progression into work.

- The partnership between Inca and a college financed by specific short-term funding was successful in supporting learners in their transition from education to employment. Further development and consolidation of the transition to work provision needed secure funding and a partnership where all parties were prepared to be equally committed in the long term.

- For people with learning difficulties, voluntary work is an important route out from education and day centres and into the community. Volunteering can provide the opportunity to learn about particular jobs and the skills involved. This could potentially equip individuals to move onto paid employment, should they wish.

Checklist

★ What links do you have with the Employment Service and could they be developed to support transition to work provision?

★ What expertise do you have within your staff team that could be used in transition to work provision?

★ What contacts does your organisation have, at governance or senior management level, with companies that may be of help to your learners/trainees?

Chapter 4 looks at the issues emerging from the project fieldwork visits and suggests ways effective transition to work provision could be developed.

References

Croydon Education Business Partnership (1996) *STATUS at WORK Pack*, Croydon Education Business Partnership

Planning and funding transition to work provision

4

This chapter examines some of things that need to be considered when planning transition to work provision. It looks at key features that emerged during the project that underpin the development of effective provision.

Researching the local employment situation

The very nature of transition to work provision dictates that staff involved in its development have to look wider than what is taught in the classroom or training centre. Information about the local employment situation, into which individuals will be making their transition, can be used to shape provision. A member of staff at a supported employment agency commented:

'Often the college courses are not relevant to the jobs available in the locality. For example, ICT courses teach students how to use computers but the jobs available need people to solve problems with computers and fix them. People who set up the courses should know what work is available.'

Researching the kind of work available locally gives transition to work provision a focus on specific skills that are in demand by employers. Learners will then have a more informed choice of actual employment opportunities that they can work towards. This makes the transition into employment much more of a reality. Supported employment organisations can be in a good position to do this research as they will already have knowledge of the local situation and links with employers, businesses and other relevant organisations. The earlier the work is done in making this match, the more focussed the transition can be. However, it is important to remember to balance this with the choices and aspirations of individual learners.

Case study

Buckinghamshire Agency for Supported Employment (BASE) works in close partnership with Amersham and Wycombe College. Together they developed a Retail Basic Skills module for people with learning difficulties or disabilities. This was in response to research through a local independent advocacy organisation and their work with disabled people in the county. The research showed a need for direct work-related basic skills training. They also knew that Buckinghamshire has an increasing skills shortage in retail businesses in the area.

Working in partnership

'Effective partnership working by all agencies is the key to achieving social inclusion for people with learning difficulties.'
(DoH Publications, 2001a)

Working in partnership with other organisations was a core feature of all the provision visited as part of the research for this pack. Many education courses have links with outside organisations, however partnership working is more than this. It is a way of joint planning and funding to ensure a seamless process for the transition to work. Effective transition to work provision will not develop unless agencies work together. Several staff who were interviewed for the project commented on the importance of partnership working:

> 'Good working relationships with other agencies are key for us.'

> 'We work in true partnership, it is difficult to see where one organisation begins and the other ends.'

> 'The relationship the college has built with the supported employment service is crucial to the success of the project and I envisage it will develop even further.'

Working in partnership with other organisations provides the opportunity to pool different areas of expertise and resources.

Case study

Bolton Community Education Services (CES) works closely with Bolton Employment Support Team (BEST). Staff and learners at Bolton CES look to BEST, with their detailed knowledge of issues around employment and people with learning difficulties, for support with the transition to work. Meanwhile, BEST values the discipline and input of education staff in relation to issues such as timekeeping, a sense of responsibility, self-presentation and social skills, which are all important in preparation for work.

Case study

Loughborough Volunteer Centre works in partnership with Rawlings Community College, Loughborough Further Education College and a local Social Services day centre. The Volunteer Centre provides voluntary work placements for people with learning difficulties from the college. People with learning difficulties have the opportunity to make the transition from day care or education to community involvement.

The Centre Co-ordinator explained:

'Partnership working allows the Volunteer Centre access to more information about an individual and their specific development plan. The transition from education to community is made easier by voluntary work placements arranged and supported whilst in education and then maintained after leaving.'

What does a partnership need to provide?

A good partnership for effective transition to work provision needs to have the capacity to be able to offer the following things:

- A relevant course or training
- Shared resources
- Links with employers who can offer work experience placements and permanent jobs
- Work experience placements where both the employer and employee are supported
- Ongoing support for the individual during and after the transition to work for as long as is appropriate
- Access to specialist knowledge about benefits and issues around employment and people with learning difficulties (for more information on benefits see chapter 5).

The partnership arrangements between organisations running and developing transition to work provision were varied. The list below details the types of partners involved in the provision that was visited for the Making the Jump project:

- Further education colleges
- Adult and community education services
- Supported employment agencies
- Volunteer centres
- Day centres
- Employers
- Self-advocacy organisations
- Disability Employment Advisors
- Parents and carers
- Benefits office
- Employment Service
- Job Centre Plus
- Social Services
- Connexions.

Whilst this list is not definitive, it does illustrate the range and type of partners that are involved in transition to work provision. There may be some different organisations in your own area, not on this list, that could have a role to play in a partnership.

Establishing links with other organisations

The project research found that the initial approaches to other organisations were sometimes down to the efforts of enthusiastic individuals or groups of staff who recognised the need to develop transition to work provision. In other cases links were developed in a more formal manner as part of a service strategy for developing day services for people with learning difficulties. Where provision was more securely established senior mangers from the different organisations had been involved in the development of partner-ships from the start.

Any multi-agency work will involve staff in ongoing liaison work with colleagues from other organisations. Support from senior managers is key so that staff have sufficient time to carry out this work.

Case study

At one college there was concern at the lack of progression of people with learning difficulties. Key individuals in the learning support department were aware of the supported employment movement and used their knowledge and enthusiasm to set up transition provision for work and other opportunities. They ran a conference, invited all the relevant senior managers; these included managers from the college itself, officers from the Local Authority Social Services and Health Authority managers. There were some fortunate outcomes since a senior Social Services Department person had previously been involved in the college and recognised many of the learners even after a gap of some years, underlining the lack of progression. Transition provision was developed in partnership with Social Services with a grant from the Local Authority.

Join Investment Plans (JIPs)

The process of developing the JIPs for Welfare to Work for Disabled People (see chapter 7) have in some cases provided a useful forum for local councils to develop links with other organisations. Most of the staff interviewed for the project were aware of the Welfare to Work JIP. Some staff had a cautious optimism about the potential of the Welfare to Work JIP to support them in the development of their provision, through its emphasis on partnership working and perhaps as a way of unlocking existing resources, to the benefit of supported employment services.

Case study

In Bolton, the development of the Welfare to Work JIP involved community consultation. The views of all people with a disability were central to the development of the Welfare to Work JIP. People with disabilities clearly stated that they were categorically in favour of employment in ordinary settings.

Bolton Community College staff were involved in planning meetings for their local JIP. They were able to highlight, through the JIP planning process, the importance of:

- Liaison work with learners and relevant organisations to enable progression for people with disabilities into work
- Continuing the expansion of services offered by BEST for vocational training, leading to work placements and then onto employment
- Recognising the importance of voluntary work for some individuals
- The continuation of the links between education, Social Services and careers, and the development of multi-agency working.

The college was the lead agency in a sub group for the Welfare to Work JIP, looking at increased opportunities for educational/ vocational training and more joint working with BEST, Lifetime Careers, New Deal and other agencies.

Working with staff from other organisations

'We are equal partners.'

'We have taken everybody with us; the students feel very positive, this keeps everybody on their toes.'

A number of different approaches to joint working were evident in examples of transition to work provision. A recent study conducted an audit of multi-agency working (Atkinson, Wilken, Stott, 2001). In the report key factors are identified that made joint-working initiatives successful. For successful multi-agency work there has to be:
- Commitment or willingness
- Good working relationships
- Leadership or drive
- Focus
- Common aims
- Funding or resources
- Involvement of relevant people
- Recognised need
- Clarity
- Joint ownership
- Information sharing
- Trust
- Understanding of roles and responsibilities.

The three key points for the successful development of joint transition to work between partner organisations, as prioritised by one manager, are:
- *'Having teams in place that are constantly flexible, tight and countywide'*
- *'Money, bringing it all together, is a gel'*
- *'Engaging the right people'*.

A member of the same team, but not in a managerial role, listed as her main reasons for successful working with partners to develop provision:

'The commitment and very clear aim of a team that is all on board. We are successful because we have outcomes, we are actually moving forward. We are driven by the needs and aspirations of the students.'

The points below were recommendations by staff as ways of working that helped develop and maintain good working relationships with colleagues from other organisations.

- Involving all partners in the planning and reviewing of provision to give everyone an understanding of the complete process an individual will be experiencing in their transition to employment. Each organisation can identify the part they play and at what stage in the process it is most appropriate for their particular expertise to be available.

- Involving at least two people in each partnership organisation in order to ensure continuity in the work. This means that if one staff member moves on there is someone left to carry on the work.

- Regular, formal meetings between the partner organisations involved in the provision.

- Running events such as open days or conferences can be a very positive way of celebrating joint work. Businesses that have provided work experience or employment are pleased to be able to have the opportunity for good publicity.

- Staff from supported employment organisations stressed that the earlier they were involved in the planning of the transition process, the easier it was for them to do their job. At an early stage in the planning of provision they are in a good position to give advice and information about the local employment situation, find relevant work experience placements, develop their plan of support for the individual and find employment opportunities. It was frustrating for them if they were involved in planning transition programmes with colleagues in education at too late a stage. This was usually when the course was already well underway.

Funding sustainable transition to work provision

There is no single obvious standard funding source for transition to work provision. This lack of statutory funding is obviously a major barrier against the development of courses and training that lead onto work. However, as this pack testifies, transition to work provision does exist in continuing education.

The provision researched for this project was funded in a variety of ways. The type of funding depended on several factors:

- The structure of the provision
- Specific funding opportunities available in the local area
- The initiative of key individuals involved.

The shared common feature of the funding at all the sites visited was that all or a proportion of the funding for transition to work provision was short term.

Sources of funding

No specific funding stream covered all aspects of the transition to work provision visited as part of the Making the Jump project. Pooling resources from several different sources was essential. The Making the Jump project found that transition to work provision had been funded by the sources listed below.

Post-16 education funding

- The change from the Further Education Funding Council (FEFC) to the Learning and Skills Council (LSC) and the amalgamation of the Training and Enterprise Council (TEC) into the Learning and Skills Council (LSC, see chapter 7) happened during the Making the Jump – Transition to work project after most of the fieldwork visits had taken place. Therefore the FEFC funded the training and education component of most of the transition to work provision based in adult and further education. The FEFC-funded courses included vocational profiling, skills training and supported work experience.

- In one case a college used its Additional Support Budget from the FEFC to pay for a contract with a local supported employment agency. The agency helped people find work and supported them in their jobs.

- Several courses used ASDAN Workright accreditation to draw down funding for students. Work funded by the LSC does not need to be externally accredited but staff did find the ASDAN framework a useful way of measuring learner achievement.

- In order to access FEFC funding one college had designed its own format for Individual Learning Programmes (ILPs) that specified that the learner's '...*Primary Learning Goal should relate to a recognised progression route as explained in Schedule 2j; FEFC circ, 99/00'*.

- One college funded additional support hours for people on transition to work provision from the Learning Support budget.

The LSCs

- The LSC funds all post-16 education provision. In addition to the core grant, the 47 local LSCs allocate money to spend on work that they have identified is a specific priority in their locality. In the autumn of 2001 a trust involved in developing services for people with learning difficulties was awarded a grant from its local LSC. The grant was to support vocational profiling work with people with learning difficulties.

New Deal for Disabled People
- A 10-week transition programme run by a college and supported employment agency was funded as a pilot for the New Deal for Disabled People.
- A community education service in a pilot area for New Deal for Disabled People Personal Advisors was able to access additional resources for transition to work provision.

Government Employment Service
- In one area a college runs a work preparation course for people with disabilities under contract to the Employment Service.

Local Authority Social Services Departments
- Several of the supported employment agencies that work in partnership with education providers are funded by the local Social Services Department.
- Social Services Departments' own employment services work in partnership with colleges and adult and community education to deliver transition to work provision.

Other sources of funding
- In one area the Lifelong Learning Partnership was making a contribution to the funding of a supported employment agency involved in transition to work provision with colleges.

Businesses
- A grant from British Gas enabled a supported employment agency to work with a college for a limited period of time, supporting people into employment.

European Social Fund (ESF)
- Grants from Europe funded the work of several of the supported employment agencies and joint work with education providers.

Working with parents

> *'Knowing your family is behind you, you've got the confidence to get a job.'*

> *'Family carers would like to see a change in the culture of services that currently cause them so much stress and often labels them as the "problem" rather than seeing them as important allies in the support of a particular person with learning difficulties.'*
> (DoH Publications, 2001b)

Support from parents, or carers, is often a key part of enabling individuals to go out to work. A parent's belief in their son or daughter's ability to hold down a job can do a huge amount for the individual's self-esteem. Practical help with getting up and out of the house on time, and transport to work, are also important. However, *'when parents say no'*, was identified by a group of people with learning difficulties in a self-advocacy organisation, as one of the main barriers to being able to get a job. Parents may find the idea of their son or daughter working as challenging for several reasons, as shown below.
- Going out to work is not as 'safe' as attending a day centre or college in terms of security and predictability. There are opportunities but there are also risks involved.
- An individual's benefits are often taken as part of total family income. If a person goes to work this may well have an affect on the whole family picture. This can be a worrying prospect for parents or carers as they may end up with less money.

- Having a job is a powerful statement of independence and as such can be a difficult thing to accept as part of the 'letting go' process.
- Work may not previously have been suggested as an option for their son or daughter, it may come as a shock that this could be a reality.
- Parents may not accept that their son or daughter has the skills to go out to work.

Parents need to be a key part of transition to work planning for their son or daughter and as such have to be appropriately involved at all relevant stages. At one further education college parents of learners are involved in the development of their son's or daughter's action plans. As one college member of staff commented:

'Parents need to feel that there is a system of support, they need liaison points, safety nets and a named person to refer to. It is important to make sure families are happy and know what a person is doing.'

The Manager of a supported employment agency stressed that it was important to:

'Make sure that parents and carers are on board and understand what is happening.'

Summary

- Information about the local employment situation, balanced with the learners' choices, can be used to shape provision and helps to make transition to work a reality.
- Working in partnership with other organisations is key to the development of effective transition to work provision. A variety of different kinds of partnership arrangements, with a range of organisations, is apparent in the examples of provision visited as part of the Making the Jump project.

- The quality of the partnership working was a more significant factor than which organisations were actually involved.
- The involvement of senior mangers and the use of formal planning processes can be very helpful with establishing links and developing partnership arrangements with other organisations.
- Clear, shared aims, good communication and the close involvement of partner organisations in the process of developing provision helps to maintain good working relationships with colleagues from other organisations.
- There is no set funding template for transition to work provision and funding can come from a variety of sources. Providers have to be creative and flexible in their approach to funding transition to work provision.
- The support of parents and carers is key to enabling individuals to go out to work. Therefore, parents and carers are an important part of any partnership when developing effective provision. They need to be kept informed and involved in the planning of the transition process for their son or daughter.
- The development of Welfare to Work JIPs can act as a catalyst for partnership formation and strategic planning by partners for transition to work provision.

Checklist

Researching the local employment situation

★ How can you find out about employment opportunities for people with learning difficulties in your area?

★ Who is best placed to develop new or existing links with local employers that could link into transition to work provision, and how can you work with them?

Working in partnership

★ Who are the key organisations in your area that could form a partnership to develop transition to work provision?

★ Is education involved in the development of the Welfare to Work JIP in your area?

★ How can you involve senior managers in your plans to develop provision?

Funding

★ What potential sources of funding are available in your area for the development of transition to work provision?

★ Which organisations could you approach to explore developing joint funding arrangements for transition to work provision?

Parents and carers

★ How can you involve parents and carers in the development of transition to work provision?

★ How will you keep them informed?

★ What support might you need to offer parents and carers?

The next chapter provides an outline of the rules and regulations regarding benefits and their effect on earnings.

References

Atkinson M, Wilken A, Stott A, *et al.* (2001) *Multi-Agency Working: An audit of activity*, LGA educational research programme, NFER

DoH Publications (2001a) *Valuing People: A new strategy for learning disability for the 21st century*, Department of Health Publications

DoH Publications (2001b) *Family Matters: Counting families in, report from the Family Carers Sub Group for Valuing People*, Department of Health Publications

Benefits

5

'We want our own money for working, real wages not benefits.'

'I can't earn too much because the government takes the money off us.'

'I have got problems at the moment but it is being sorted out. They owe me some money. They took it because of the work that I am doing, but then I shouldn't have done that.'

It is very apparent that fear of being worse off working than on benefits acts as a significant deterrent to looking for work for people with learning difficulties, their families and often professionals who work with them.

This is not surprising. The system of benefits in the UK is immensely complex and can, in a minority of cases, mean that a person is worse off when working. The administration is also often confused and inconsistent with people getting different advice in different parts of the country. However, it is still the case that many people with learning difficulties who receive benefits can still be better off working, although this requires detailed, specialist support from people who really understand the system.

Case study

Buckinghamshire Agency for Supported Employment (BASE) uses a computer programme to work out the affect that peoples' earnings will have on their benefits. This work is done as part of an individual's assessment process with the student and college staff. The database is updated regularly and benefit liaison meetings take place every 3 months. A member of staff at BASE, who previously worked for the Benefits Agency, leads this work.

Those on disability benefits

Most people with learning difficulties will be on one, or a combination, of the three benefits listed below.

- Incapacity Benefit (IB): a taxable, means-tested benefit for those seen as being 'incapable' of work, only paid to those who have contributed sufficient National Insurance contributions.
- Severe Disablement Allowance (SDA): a benefit for people seen as being 'incapable of work' but who do not have enough National Insurance contributions to qualify for IB (SDA is going to be abolished for young people coming into the system).
- Income Support (IS): designed to ensure that all people have enough income to provide for basic living costs. This benefit automatically triggers other benefits such as free prescriptions and automatic access to maximum applicable rates of Housing and Council Tax Benefits.

In addition people with learning difficulties might receive Disabled Living Allowance (DLA), which is divided into a care component and a mobility component, and can be paid at different levels.

It is possible to be on disability benefits and earn some money (see the permitted work rules below), however there are limits to what you can earn. For IB and SDA the limit is currently £66. The rules for IS are more complicated: the initial £20 of earnings are 'disregarded' for benefit purposes; after that IS is reduced by £1 for each extra £1 earned, until the point at which either the permitted work limits are reached, or the person is no longer eligible for IS.

The national minimum wage

'I would like to work more hours and earn more pay.'

All workers are entitled to the national minimum wage. However, for people with learning difficulties who are earning a maximum of £20 a week, this has had the effect of restricting the number of hours they can work. There is a balance to be struck between spreading the work over as many hours as an individual may choose to work and not exploiting an individual by paying them below the national minimum wage. You might want to check with the Department for Trade and Industry (DTI) for guidance.

Therapeutic work and new permitted work rules

Those receiving IB and SDA (and IS claimed on the basis of incapacity) have been able to undertake 'therapeutic work' that does not affect their benefits. This could not be undertaken without a letter from a doctor stating that the work will in some way benefit a person's condition. Therapeutic work could not exceed 16 hours a week (unless they lived in residential care) and an individual could not earn more than £66 a week. Although this income does not affect benefits there is often a concern that it might trigger a review of eligibility to benefits.

From 8th April 2002 therapeutic work is being replaced by new permitted work rules. Under these rules people will be able to work for less than 16 hours a week with earnings of up to £66 a week for a 26-week period. This period can be extended for another 26 weeks if a person is working with a Job Broker, Personal Advisor or Disability Employment Advisor, who agrees that it will help towards work of more than 16 hours a week.

No one will have to undergo a medical test just because they are doing permitted work.

Supported work

The new rulings also cover supported work. They allow special arrangements for those disabled people who are being supported into work. People, such as those with learning difficulties, whose condition is unlikely to improve over time, will continue to be able to indefinitely combine some work (less than 16 hours a week, earning less than £66 a week) with receiving their incapacity benefits.

Under the new rules people who work in the community with ongoing support or supervision from a professional caseworker (employed or engaged by a public body or voluntary organisation) will not be subject to time limits. The new category will be called 'supported work' and will include, for example, people who:

- Are employed by Social Firms via support centres
- Are in touch with a Care Co-ordinator or Employment Development Officer
- Have had a Social Services Assessment.

This new ruling is intended to help those people whose disability means their working capacity is limited to less than 16 hours a week but who can work more than the few hours covered by the £20 option.

Disabled Person's Tax Credit (DPTC)

When a person works for more than 16 hours a week their benefits will begin to taper off, although an individual should retain their DLA. However, they might lose some of the other benefits that come with IS.

If they are working more than 16 hours a week but on a low income they may be eligible for DPTC which could supplement their earnings and compensate for loss of benefits.

If a person's job fails and they wish to return to the benefits they had before, in theory there is a right to a return to the same level of benefit for up to 1 year and for up to 2 years for those who have been receiving DPTC. In practice such a return can take some time to happen and there is also a fear that because a person has worked, their entitlement to benefits may be reviewed.

Those only on IS

If a person with a learning difficulty is only receiving IS they are able to earn up to £20 a week without their benefit being affected. After that they will normally move directly onto part-time work. If they work for more than 16 hours a week they will be eligible for DPTC.

Some young people with learning difficulties might be getting Job Seekers' Allowance (JSA). If this is the case they will have to prove that they are actively looking for work.

Those in residential care

There is a particular issue for those in residential care who find employment as this means that they will then have to start contributing to the costs of their placement. Because the cost of residential care is so great it is very unlikely that a person in residential care can ever gain financial benefit from paid employment. Local Authorities do have the discretion to allow residents to keep all or a proportion of their earnings, but it appears that few of them exercise this discretion.

The summary above provides a very brief outline of what is a very complex set of rules and regulations. Each individual will need to be assessed separately to see how a move into work affects him or her.

Neverthless, it is also apparent that many people with learning difficulties can be better off financially if they are working than if they are unemployed.

> 'I still get my DLA and that is not affected by working. I used to get IS and SDA but not anymore. I don't get DPTC as I earn too much, but that is OK.'

The major messages that have come across during this project have been:
- The need for individuals to get expert advice on how their benefits will be affected by work
- The need for practitioners supporting people into employment to have close allies in the Benefits Agency

- Acknowledging that fears of losing benefits are very real, but not letting those fears prevent a clear appraisal of an individual's situation.

The next chapter outlines the key components of a curriculum for transition to work provision.

References

O'Bryan A, Simons K, Beyer S, *et al*. (2000) *Economic Security and Supported Employment*, National Development Team
For information on the national minimum wage and therapeutic earnings see: www.dti.gov.uk-er-nmw-therapeutic.pdf.url

Learning and work – the curriculum for transition to work

6

Case study

'College courses helped me get a Basic Food Hygiene Certificate, and the NVQ course gave me the confidence to want a job. It also helped me to make new friends. Judith, from the Employment Support Team, came to the interview with me and then supported me in the job for the first 3 weeks. I now don't need any support, and I am paid for the work I do.'

This chapter focuses on different elements of the curriculum for transition to work courses. As the quote above illustrates, transition to work provision offers individuals the opportunity to:

- Learn vocational skills
- Gain qualifications
- Go on work experience
- Grow in confidence
- Develop interpersonal skills
- Have support in finding a job
- Have one-to-one support in the workplace as appropriate.

A group of adults with learning difficulties involved in voluntary work were asked what they had learnt that helped them in their work:

' Learning to travel on your own.'

'Health and safety training.'

'Courses about ways to work and making choices when you are working.'

'Margaret helped me learn about the dishwasher.'

'I did food hygiene at college.'

Different ways transition to work curricula are organised

Transition is a period of development and movement, in this context: from being a learner/trainee to an employee. Individuals' needs will change during the transition to work process. A transition to work curriculum has to be flexible so it can respond to these changing needs. There are different models of curriculum design, but all curricula must, in some form, include an identification of need, decisions about curriculum content and delivery, and methods of evaluation. However this chapter does not attempt to create a model for a transition to work curriculum. Individual decisions will need to be made depending on several factors, in particular the type of students it is for and the resources that are available. What this chapter does is looks at certain elements that are likely to be important factors in any transition to work curriculum.

Identifying need and initial planning

Identifying need
In any initial planning for a transition to work curriculum it is essential to start by identifying the aims and aspirations that people with learning difficulties have in relation to employment. It is also essential to research local employment opportunities (as discussed in chapter 4).

Partnership working and curriculum design
As the examples in other chapters show, partnership working is crucial for transition to work provision. The involvement of other agencies will have an impact on the curriculum and this needs to be taken into account when the curriculum is being developed. A joint meeting with other agencies involved in the provision could discuss:

- The aims and objectives of the curriculum
- The particular areas of expertise of partner organisations
- How and what stage this expertise can most effectively be included in the curriculum
- Initial ideas for possible sharing of resources.

Curriculum content

This section looks at elements that are likely to be particularly important in a transition to work curriculum.

Interpersonal skills

'The best bit is in the warehouse because I work with the team.'

'We did a role-play where someone is complaining that they have been overcharged.'

' Some people would like a job but they have a fear of going for it … frightened to go out to work because of the reactions of others.'

'I would like to have part-time paid work but I need a lot of reassurance. Being at college, mixing in a big building and meeting new people has helped my confidence.'

The ability to get on with colleagues at work is a key part of most jobs. People with learning difficulties may often have spent much time socialising in segregated environments such as day centres or on discrete college and adult education courses. Developing interpersonal skills is a core part of a transition to work curriculum. Being at college with others learners can provide some opportunities to develop these skills as can work experience placements.

Case study

As a result of a request from Bolton Employment Support Team (BEST), Bolton Community College has started a course focusing on the interpersonal and social skills needed for successful employment, rather than training specifically in a vocational area.

By not being vocationally directed, it was felt that the Skills for Work course could be planned and delivered in partnership with BEST to best meet the needs of learners. The experience and expertise of BEST in supporting people in the workplace brings an added dimension to the course, which is part of an employment-training programme at the college. Service users who are working, employers and college tutors are also involved in the delivery of the course. Before the conclusion of the course, learners will be involved in work placements, organised and supported by BEST. The course runs for 3 terms, 2.5 days a week. Areas covered include:

- Teamwork – looking at the skills needed to be valued member of a team, using group-work projects to experience teamwork through planning and practical activities
- Confidence-building and assertiveness
- Considering the advantages/disadvantages of work
- Personal presentation
- Interview skills
- Looking at the skills individuals already have
- Exploring jobs people do and identifying help and support that may be needed
- How to deal with problems that occur at work
- Workplace visits.

Vocational skills

> 'I wanted to learn new skills, like stock control, and work for a big company. You learn about different jobs, like how you would act when giving refunds. It is a good way of improving your confidence.'

One of the main tenets of the supported employment movement is '… that the workplace is the best place to learn a job'. As one tutor said, 'make sure what we do is real, we mustn't simulate. It is no good digging and planting in the classroom rather than outside'.

A vocational curriculum that combines classroom-based learning with work experience, which can then develop on to employment, is crucial if learners are to make the transition to work. The involvement of a supported employment agency can make this a reality.

A manager at Amersham and Wycombe college explained that the development of the college vocational provision with Buckinghamshire Agency for Supported Employment (BASE):

> '… brought all our efforts alive, a chance for a person to take on a job and make a success of it… We can get away from classroom-based activities into a stimulating new environment to learn skills. This changed the whole curriculum offer to having an enterprise theme. We feel confident to do that through collaboration with BASE. The creation of the BASE connection turns progression into a reality.'

Case study

In its work with Croydon College, STATUS Employment Agency use the *STATUS at WORK* pack. The pack was originally developed to be used with two local schools. A number of teachers went on placements in various different companies and spent half a day shadowing an employee with learning difficulties, to learn their job. This process mirrors how an Employment Consultant at STATUS would assess a job in order to support an individual in work. The teachers who had been on the placements then wrote the teaching materials for the pack.

Ten jobs are described in the pack ranging from a Sales Assistant and a Support Technician to a Data Entry Clerk and a Catering Assistant. An accompanying photo pack contains pictures of people with learning difficulties carrying out various tasks in their jobs. There are various activities for learners that illustrate the skills needed for a particular job. The learning objectives of the materials are to:

- Be aware of the different types of work they can take up
- Know about the tasks associated with different jobs
- Understand that different jobs require different skills
- Improve their understanding of the social norms of the workplace
- Become more familiar with the work-related vocabulary of the workplace
- Learn about matters related to work such as making journeys, time management and managing money.

Literacy and numeracy

At the time of writing this pack basic skills are a high priority for the government. A major national programme, funded by the Department for Education and Skills (DfES), on literacy, language and numeracy for adults with learning difficulties and/or disabilities, launched a series of publications in September 2001. The publications included the *Adult Pre-entry Curriculum Framework for Literacy and Numeracy* and *Access for All*, guidance on making the adult literacy and numeracy core curricula accessible. May 2002 saw the start of a series of DfES training events across England based on the *Adult Pre-entry Curriculum Framework* and *Access for All*. The training events are for practitioners working across agencies including Education, Health, Social Services and Voluntary Organisations.

The Retail Basic Skills course at Amersham and Wycombe College is supported by various companies who give information; job descriptions; application forms; work experience log books; and health and safety details, which are adapted and used as learning materials on the course. The companies send representatives to the college to talk about jobs. Supported Employment Officers (SEOs) liaise with the college and the companies and set up work placements for people on the course.

Case study

A BASE SEO sat in on the Retail Basic Skills to observe what a particular individual was learning. After a discussion with the learner and armed with a copy of their timetable the SEO met with a supervisor at a local supermarket. The SEO talked about the strengths and skills the individual had to offer and when he could be available for work experience. Following an interview, the learner was successful in securing a work experience placement at the supermarket. The SEO supports the individual on his placement and liaises with the college to ensure the course supports him with the knowledge and basic skills he needs in the workplace. This learner has now been offered another day's work experience.

For all learners, and particularly those with learning difficulties, basic skills will be easier to learn if they are relevant to the learner's life. In Loughborough, a group of people with learning difficulties from a day centre meet in a community-based venue. A basic skills tutor comes from the local college to teach the group. The learners then go out and apply the skills they have learnt in their voluntary work placements. They explained what they do in their voluntary work:

> 'I work in the canteen... I go shopping to get the food for lunch.'

> 'I work at the Sense and Barnardo shops. I sort out clothes and work on the till. The lady in the shop showed me how to do it. Another job I do is to label 250 bags and tick a box that says if it is Monday or Thursday.'

Self-advocacy

> 'The government will work in partnership with the self-advocacy movement to promote the development of a clear national voice for people with learning disabilities.'
> (DoH, 2001)

Central to a curriculum that empowers people with learning difficulties are the principles of self-advocacy. As one person with learning difficulties explained:

> 'Self-advocacy is being able to speak up for yourself and having confidence in yourself to be able to do it.'
> (DfES, 2001)

The transition to employment from education is a major life change for the individual involved. Having a sense of control and purpose is key to helping the individual feel comfortable and confident about starting work. The involvement of people in developing and directing their own transition process is crucial. The accompanying publication to this pack, '*We can do a good job*', for people with learning difficulties who want to work, suggests ways that people can be involved in their own transition process.

When developing a transition to work curriculum, consulting with people with learning difficulties and listening to what they have to say about work and learning, can inform the process at all stages. The learner has to be central, from the initial assessment, the development of Individual Learning Programmes (ILPs) and work experience placements through to on-the-job support once the individual has 'made the jump'.

Equal opportunities and the transition to work curriculum

An awareness of and good practice around issues of gender, race, age and disability must be an integral part of all curriculum elements. There may be times when this means making specific provision for specific groups of learners.

Case study

Amersham and Wycombe College runs a practical work skills course for Asian women with learning difficulties. The course is only for women in order to meet the cultural needs of this particular group of learners. The course takes place on the main college campus so the learners can choose to mix with other people at the college if they want. A Punjabi-speaking assistant works alongside the course tutor. The women on the course are supported in discussing and planning their progression by Talkback Self Advocacy, a local independent self-advocacy organisation.

A recent report (Foundation for People with Learning Disabilities, 2000) highlights ways in which the methods used in supported employment have been successfully adapted to work with '*people with learning disabilities and high support needs*'. This group of learners are under-represented in continuing education but there are some examples of provision, as discussed in the NIACE publication, *All Things Being Equal?* (Sutcliffe and Jacobsen 1998).

Qualifications

> '*I went to a course that helped us with a NVQ in Business Admin. I found parts of it were quite easy to do because of experience from previous jobs. There was an awful lot of evidence-based work. For what I learnt, the work we had to do to get the qualification was really tough. If you had gone on the course straight from school I think it would have been easier because everything would be new. The amount of work we were asked to do was incredible considering it was so basic.*'

There are different views on the importance of qualifications for people with learning difficulties, whose primary wish is to gain employment. There is currently a lot of government pressure on colleges to ensure that as many learners as possible gain qualifications. However, there were concerns from one supported employment agency that a particular college was over selling its training. Some college marketing materials can suggest that the acquisition of an NVQ is a passport to employment, whereas in reality this is often not the case, particularly in the case of people with learning difficulties.

One supported employment agency recognised the value of NVQs, particularly in the development of self-respect. However, they also felt that few employers value the qualification in its own right, preferring to judge employees on their ability to complete the tasks assigned them. One employer was very clear that NVQs were a part of the training regime for all employees and that, for the person placed with them, having an NVQ 1 was seen as an advantage.

Curriculum designers need to make choices, based on individual's learning plans, as to which targets are most relevant for each individual learner. The ASDAN Workright accreditation was being used by several of the places visited as part of the fieldwork for the Making the Jump project. Staff valued the flexibility of this particular accreditation scheme and adapted it to suit the needs of their learners. It is important to remember however, that as an accreditation scheme it does not provide curriculum content and it is not appropriate to use it as a curriculum for transition to work provision.

Curriculum delivery

Although there are certain elements of work preparation that might very successfully be taught to a group of learners, any curriculum that is designed to support individuals into a job will have to ensure a high degree of individual planning and delivery.

Individual planning

> *'The key thing is to find out at the start of the course what area of employment the student is interested in.'*

> *'You need to be sure it is the job you want to go for.'*

A transition to work curriculum that is shaped by ILPs links in well with the personalised nature of supported employment. Staff can work with a learner to develop their own transition 'package' based on their particular needs. As a planning tool ILPs can and are being used for learners with different levels of need. At Amersham and Wycombe College, ILPs are used as the basis for an action plan

that is reviewed 6 times a year with all learners. Parents and carers
also share in the action plans.

Case study

At Joseph Priestley College people on the Access to Community and Employment
Course have training packages based on ILPs. The ILP portfolio focuses on:

- What kind of work a learner is interested in
- Identifying the skills that a learner has and ways of developing these skills
- Looking at the new skills a learner needs to develop
- What the learners are aiming to achieve.

At the first stage of the course, each person has a vocational profile and an
external specialist appraises welfare benefits and financial issues. In parallel with
the college-based learning, approaches are being made to employers to provide
training placements.

In the second stage of the course problem solving is addressed, relating to any
skills development that the individual might need and building support networks
around them, both in the workplace and the home. For example, one person on
work experience in a fish and chip restaurant was being asked to start preparing
the chicken for frying and to mix the coleslaw. The proprietor was asked to write
out their methods for the tasks so that they could be reinforced in the college's
catering department. They were written into the learner's ILP. When additional
tasks are being negotiated all those involved regard the resources available at the
college as an asset.

The third stage of the course sees the learner formally employed, with the
introduction of a contract of employment, and changes in their benefit claim. This
stage is expected to last 18 weeks and over this period any problems arising from
this change in status are addressed, as are any other training issues. The learner's

---

ILP sets learning goals that are of parallel benefit to their learning and employment requirements.

The fourth stage sees the transition from learner to employee complete and there is no longer a need to have formal links to the college at this stage. Responsibility for continued support to both employee and employer is handed over to a partner agency that continues until such time as the job comes to a conclusion.

Case study

Members of the Workwise course at Blackburn College have ILPs based on the ASDAN Workright package. Learners work one-to-one with a tutor for an hour on the portfolio for the ASDAN course. They also have a support hour linked in with their work placement. The course co-ordinator is the internal verifier for the ASDAN course. She visits the work placement regularly to liaise with the employer and to assess the learner. There is the flexibility to build in other classes, e.g. Basic Skills, part of an NVQ, First Aid. Individuals can attend the session with or without support, depending on what is most appropriate.

April to July is the transition period when people exit college. The aim is to try to secure a job either at the place where the individual has been on placement or something similar. Then the supported employment organisation will take over the support. Some learners go onto do voluntary work.

Basing a curriculum on ILPs is a very different approach from the way that many further and adult education curricula are designed. It marks a significant change of culture in regard to achievement and reaching targets. Staff who prefer a traditional approach to teaching can be critical of ILPs and they may resist working with them. However, the recent government White Paper, *Valuing People*, emphasises very strongly the importance of individual planning for people with learning difficulties. If education providers are to work with other agencies in order to create a holistic programme for people with learning difficulties they need to look at ways of developing an individualised approach to teaching and learning.

A further challenge to working with ILPs is that learners' courses can be individualised to such an extent that they lose any opportunity to mix and socialise with their peers, as one tutor explained:

> *'Students on the course never meet as they are either on their work placement or working with a tutor on their ASDAN portfolio.'*

This absence of peer-group support could be counter productive for learners. Some projects have found different ways of ensuring that people do continue to benefit from peer-group support, as shown below.

Case study

In Buckinghamshire, the groups that Talkback Self Advocacy run can be a form of peer support as people can lose contact with friends when they leave college and go to work.

Case study

The 'Free Time' group was set up in Croydon so that people with learning difficulties who were going out to work did not become isolated and lose their peer support. The group meets at a room in the town hall. People have the chance to meet up on a regular basis with friends for a chat.

Evaluation

Evaluation of the transition to work curriculum needs to happen at all stages; both during and after the course, and should always involve learners.

Course evaluation needs to be both quantitative and qualitative. It must of course include an analysis of how many students actually did make the jump into paid employment. However, it is essential that it also analyses the extent to which an individual's quality of life has been enhanced.

Work can be a reality for a lot of people with learning difficulties. It may be a small but important part of an individual's life and a way of contributing to the community. It may be a big part of an individual's life and daily activity. There are people with learning difficulties working as freelance trainers/consultants and people with learning difficulties who are involved in a day of voluntary work each week or a few hours of paid work each week.

Case study

Bert is in his fifties. He has been in residential care for most of his life and in recent years has attended a day centre. He has a talent for fine art. A few years ago he was on the Workwise programme; he had a work placement at a local community arts group, worked towards Workright accreditation, and attended Adult Basic Skills sessions at college. The staff at the work placement were so impressed that they asked him to remain working there on a voluntary basis. He is still going there for 1 day a week. He has been able to secure several 'commissions' for the art group.

Summary

- A curriculum for transition to work has to be flexible and responsive in order to support learners through a period of significant change. ILPs are a particularly effective way of designing programmes to support learners in their transition to work.

- People with learning difficulties may have had limited opportunities to mix in a range of social settings. Relating to and communicating well with colleagues is an important part of most jobs. Support with interpersonal skills as part of a transition to work curriculum is key.

- Relating vocational, literacy and numeracy skills to the practical tasks undertaken on work placements or work tasters is an important component of a transition to work curriculum.

- At the time of the Making the Jump project the government was supporting a major training programme for staff working across agencies, based on the *Adult Pre-Entry Curriculum Framework for Literacy and Numeracy*. Developing literacy and numeracy skills in the context of the workplace can be a key part of a curriculum for transition to work.

- Partner organisations involved in transition to work provision should be consulted on the content and development of the curriculum.

- Incorporating the principles and skills of self-advocacy throughout the curriculum is a key way of empowering individuals in their transition to work.

- The development of a curriculum for transition to work has to take into account equal opportunities issues, including differing abilities, gender, race and age.

Checklist

★ How can you develop effective ILPs that will be flexible and responsive?

★ How will you involve partner organisations in the development of a transition to work curriculum?

★ How will you make self-advocacy an integral part of the transition to work curriculum?

Learners' comments

This chapter concludes with some comments from people who have made the transition to employment.

How was college useful?

- 'I learnt things like counting money.'
- 'The course helped me to write and spell.'
- 'It was useful going on my work experience.'
- 'It helped me do my art.'
- 'I made friends at college.'
- 'The sandwich delivery service helped me learn about money and deal with customers.'
- 'We were learning about different jobs and improving work skills.'
- 'Learning to use the computers.'

How did the Supported Employment Service help you get a job?

- 'Support with going to interviews.'
- 'Filling in the forms and checking them to make sure that they are okay.'
- 'Making a CV.'

- *'It helped me find the job I have.'*
- *'Looking at newspapers.'*
- *'I went on work experience to see if I liked the job and then I got paid.'*
- *'I get support in my job from Pathway. They come in and see me and make sure that everything is alright, and go to any meetings with me.'*

What is the best thing about your job?

- *'The people. They are actually really nice and friendly; and obviously the money as well!'*
- *'I enjoy doing it. I finish early. I get up early to do this job and I have to have a sleep when I get home.'*
- *'Taking the clients bowling.'*
- *'Helping the customers out to the car park.'*
- *'Keeping the baskets tidy for the customers.'*
- *'Keeping an eye on the express tills.'*

What advice would you give to a person with learning difficulties who is thinking about getting a job?

- *'Look at the newspapers.'*
- *'I would tell them to go to college to help them get a job.'*
- *'Go on work experience.'*
- *'Get help from Pathway or if you live in a home like me they can help you, or your parents.'*
- *'It's very hard, you just have to hang on in there and see what happens.'*
- *'The interviews have not been as bad as I thought they would be.'*

The next chapter gives an overview of policy initiatives relevant to transition to work for people with learning difficulties.

References

DoH Publications (2001) *Valuing People: A new strategy for learning disability for the 21st century*, Department of Health Publications

DfES (2001) *The Self-Advocacy Action Pack*, Department for Education and Skills

Foundation for People with Learning Disabilities (2000) *Everyday Lives, Everyday Choices for People with Learning Disabilities and High Support Needs*, Foundation for People with Learning Disabilities

Sutcliffe J and Jacobsen Y (1998) *All Things Being Equal? A practical guide to widening participation for adults with learning difficulties in continuing education*, National Institute of Adult and Continuing Education

Resources

The publications listed all relate to literacy, language and numeracy for adults with learning difficulties or disabilities. This major national programme was funded by the Department for Education and Skills and ran from September 2000 to March 2001. The work was managed by a consortium* jointly led by the Learning and Skills Development Agency and the National Institute for Adult Continuing Education.

Living our Lives

Ten Readers written by learners for learners. They are the life stories of ten people with learning difficulties, offering a resource for learners and tutors. They come with an audio CD.

(2001, Prolog reference: LOL)

The Self Advocacy Action Pack

A pack written for adults with learning difficulties on speaking up and self-advocacy. This comes with an audio CD.
(2001, Prolog reference: SAAP)

Yesterday I Never Stopped Writing

Guidance on developing community-based basic skills provision for adults with learning difficulties or disabilities. It is a write-up of projects funded under a short-term grants programme.
(2001, Prolog reference: YNSW)

Skills Explorer BSL

A CD ROM of practical literacy activities for BSL users at Entry level.
(2002, Prolog reference: SEBSL)

Skills Explorer

A CD ROM of practical literacy and numeracy activities for learners at Entry level.
(2001, Prolog reference: SEABS)

The above publications are available free of charge from:
DfES Publications
PO Box 5050
Sherwood Park
Annesley
Nottingham NG15 ODJ
Tel: 0845 60 222 60
Text Phone: 0845 60 555 60
Fax: 0845 60 333 60
Email: dfes@prolog.uk.com

Adult Pre-Entry Curriculum Framework for Literacy and Numeracy
Written for staff working with adults with learning difficulties.

Access for All – Guidance on making the adult literacy and numeracy core curricula accessible
Written to provide advice to staff teaching learners who have range of disabilities and learning difficulties.

The above two curriculum documents are available free of charge from:
The Basic Skills Agency
PO Box 270
Wetherby
West Yorkshire LS23 7BJ
Tel: 0870 600 2400
Fax: 0870 600 2401
Website: www.basic-skills.co.uk

* Consortium partners were Basic Skills Agency, Skill, National Bureau for Students with Disabilities, London Language and Literacy Unit, Birmingham Rathbone, Mental Health Foundation, including the Foundation for People with Learning Disabilities, Cambridge Training and Development and University for Industry.

Policy – opportunities for change

7

In recent years the government has expressed its intention that more people with disabilities or learning difficulties should be given the opportunity to enter employment. This chapter will give a brief overview of some of the policy initiatives that may support this and will then go on to look at some ways in which managers could make use of the initiatives to facilitate support into employment.

Education and training

The Learning and Skills Council (LSC)

In April 2001, the LSC took over the funding of further education, adult education and work-based training. The Learning and Skills Act 2000 lays down the duties that the LSC has to follow. It includes certain duties specifically related to disabled learners. The LSC has a duty to:

- Have regard to the needs of people with learning difficulties when providing education, training and work experience
- Have due regard to promote equality of opportunity between disabled and non-disabled people.

In addition to this, the same Act states that every school leaver with a statement of special educational needs must have a written assessment of their needs in post-school education or training.

Some other factors are also important when looking at how the development of the LSC could support learning programmes that are established to support people with learning difficulties into employment. Firstly, the fact that the LSC funds both post-school education and work-based training could be used to facilitate closer collaborative work between colleges and training organisations. Secondly, the LSC is not subject to Schedule 2 of the Further and Higher Education Act 1992. This means that Schedule 2j, which stated that students with learning difficulties could only attend further education if it would enable them to progress to another Schedule 2 learning programme, no longer applies. There is therefore no legal restriction against colleges offering courses for students with learning difficulties that have other outcomes, such as employment. Finally, the Department for Education and Skills (DfES) has issued *Guidance to the Learning and Skills Council on meeting the needs of learners with learning difficulties and disabilities*. This Guidance specifically mentions the importance of learners with disabilities and learning difficulties accessing work experience. The DfES has also issued colleges and universities with specific guidelines on supporting learners with disabilities and/or learning difficulties on work experience. (DfES, 2002)

Work-based training

Up until 2001, Training and Enterprise Councils (TECs) managed work-based training. While some areas had excellent provision for trainees with learning difficulties this provision varied greatly from one geographical area to another. From April 2001 this area of work came under the management of the LSC. Work-based training includes Modern Apprenticeships and also a category called Other Training that allows training at NVQ Levels 1 and 2, and sometimes Level 3. It is Other Training that enables providers to put on training programmes for people who might not be able to gain NVQ Level 2, or will need a lot of support to do so. Recently there has been a review of work-based learning by the Modern Apprenticeship Advisory Committee that has been endorsed by the government in

November 2001. One of the outcomes of this is the planned replacement of Other Training with a new Entry to Employment (E2E). E2E is for learners who need extra time and support to access either Modern Apprenticeships or other employment. Initial E2E pathfinder projects will be starting in August 2002.

Additional support funding for learners in further education or work-based learning

Currently learners in further education who have additional support needs, on account of their disability or learning difficulty, can receive Additional Support Funding from the LSC. In work-based training provision there has been interim arrangements put in place for 2001/02, allowing learners to be assessed according to their 'Additional Learning Needs' and 'Additional Social Needs' and receive additional funding of up to £1500 over the usual fund, if it is deemed they have additional needs.

The LSC recognise the need to move towards a single definition of additional learning support across the post-16 sector and have issued a First Stage Consultation on Additional Support document (Circular 02/04, February 2002). In 2002/03 Additional Support Funding in further education colleges will continue as before but new additional support arrangements will be piloted in the work-based sector through the new E2E pathfinder projects. The intention is that by 2003/04 all parts of the post-16 sector will come under a single system of Additional Support Funding.

The Disability Discrimination Act 1995

Disabled employees are given specific rights not to be discriminated against in employment on account of their disability by the Disability Discrimination Act (DDA) 1995. This was followed by Part 3, Goods and Services, which extends these rights to the provision of goods and services. In 2001 a new Act was passed, the Special Educational Needs and Disability Act (SENDA). This Act brings education under the DDA, and becomes Part 4 of the DDA. From September 2002, colleges and Local Authorities providing post-school education will have duties:

- Not to discriminate against a person because of their disability
- To provide reasonable adjustments to ensure that disabled learners have equal access to post-school education.

The Disability Rights Commission has a duty to provide conciliation for disabled people who feel they have been unjustifiably treated because of their disability and, in the final instance, to support them in bringing a legal case against their college or Local Authority.

Social Services

The Chronically Sick and Disabled Act 1970 gives each Local Authority a duty to meet certain needs of disabled people, although several High Court rulings have stated that the Local Authority is entitled to take its resources into account when deciding what service to provide. The National Health Service and Community Care Act 1990, in conjunction with the Disabled Person's Act 1986, gives the Local Authority the duty to assess a disabled person's need for community care services.

Joint Investment Plans (JIPs)

More recently Social Services have been required to respond to the government's Welfare to Work agenda. From April 2001 all Social Services have been required to develop JIPs on their 'Welfare to Work' services, (as mentioned previously in chapter 4). Social Services have the key role but they are also required to work in partnership with a range of key agencies (Health, the Employment Service, the Benefits Agency, the LSC and the newly-forming Connexions Service). JIPs have to show how agencies plan to use their joint resources to develop and invest in services over the next 3 years.

Valuing People

In March 2001 the government issued a White Paper, *Valuing People: A new strategy for learning disability for the 21st century*. A fundamental theme underlying this paper is that people with learning difficulties should be involved in planning their own services and that services should be designed so that they can respond to the wishes and aspirations of individuals rather than individuals having to fit into predetermined services. One of the key messages of the White Paper is the need to increase the number of people with learning difficulties accessing employment. It recognises that a number of different agencies are currently involved in supporting people with learning difficulties into employment and emphasises the necessity of far closer collaboration between Social Services and these other agencies.

The White Paper also emphasises the need to increase the number of people with learning difficulties who can buy in some of their services directly through the Direct Payments Scheme. Currently the rules for this are complex and only certain services can be purchased in this way, but it has given many disabled people far more autonomy to be able to employ a support worker directly rather than be allocated someone through Social Services.

The main driver for the implementation of Valuing People will be the new Learning Disability Partnership Boards. These boards will have the responsibility of updating Learning Disability JIPs and drawing up local action plans containing proposals for implementing Valuing People. They will need to look closely at the Welfare to Work JIP to ensure that it deals adequately with the particular vocational, educational and job support needs of people with learning difficulties – for example that there are sufficient job coaching and supported employment options.

Learning Disability Partnership Boards had to be established by 31st October 2001. The Chief Executive of the local council, with responsibility for Social Services, is responsible for setting up these boards. Membership should include representatives from statutory services (including Social Services, health bodies, education, housing and the Employment Service); representatives from independent and voluntary organisations and at least two people with learning disabilities and two carers.

Major priorities for the Boards include devising a framework for introducing a person-centred approach to planning services and ensuring that as many learning disabled people as possible take part in education, training and employment.

Social Services funding for supported employment

Several Social Services Departments also fund specialist, supported employment. However, while this may work well in some areas it is far from universal.

Advice and Guidance

Connexions Service

The new Connexions Service was established in April 2001 and is being rolled out to cover all areas of England by 2003. It will provide all 13–19-year-olds with access to advice, guidance and support through the creation of a network of Personal Advisors. The Connexions Service also has the power to continue working with young people with learning difficulties or disabilities up to the age of 25. The role of Personal Advisors is to assess young people's needs and help them devise their own action plan. They will then support this action plan by linking with the range of services that might be required to support the young person. The Connexions Service, as it develops, will be a key service for supporting people with learning difficulties in their transition to employment.

The Employment Service

New Deal

New Deal has been established to support young people into employment. A Personal Adviser is allocated to each young person, whose role is to help them access the most appropriate pathway to employment. In addition to this the New Deal for Disabled People (NDDP) pilot projects have been testing a range of approaches to find out how best to help disabled people who want to work. NDDP is being extended nationally from July 2001 building on experience in the pilot phase. A central feature of this will be the development of a network of job brokers to offer work focussed to help disabled people.

Some areas of the UK have developed the role of the New Deal Personal Advisors to create a ONE service. From April 2002 ONE pilots will be becoming the new service, Job Centre Plus. ONE combines resources from the Employment Service and the Benefits Agency in order to provide a 'one-stop shop' where people could simultaneously receive advice on employment and benefit issues.

Disability Service Teams

The Employment Service also provides support to people through Job Centres and the specialist service offered by its Disability Service Teams. Disability Employment Advisors, employed by these teams, can offer support both to employers and disabled job seekers/employees. They can draw down Access to Work funding, an important funding stream that can provide practical support – for example specialist hardware, personal support or transport costs for disabled people, to help them enter and stay in employment.

Government Supported Employment Programme/Workstep

This programme is managed by the Employment Service, which contracts with 200 Local Authorities and voluntary organisations and Remploy Ltd. It provides jobs to support over 22,000 disabled people who face complex barriers to getting or keeping a job. Some of these are employed in supported factories or businesses. Many others are in subsidised employment whereby the Employment Service pays a proportion of their wage.

The Supported Employment Programme has recently been reviewed and will be going through a process of modernisation. From April 2001 it has been renamed Workstep and it will have a greater focus on helping disabled people move into mainstream employment with longer-term support available where needed. The aim for progression will be 10 per cent a year for existing supported employees and 30 per cent over 10 years for new supported employees. The evaluation of the new programme will look at its impact on people with learning difficulties. The funding model for new starts on the programme is more flexible than previously and may pay for job coaching or enable employers to have grants for mentoring or training as an alternative to wage subsidy or a factory place.

Other agencies

Not all supported employment programmes are managed by the statutory agencies mentioned above. Funding comes from a range of different sources including charitable funding sources, Single Regeneration Budget funding in England and European funding. In addition to this some areas have created social firms or social enterprises. Social firms are ordinary businesses set up to provide goods or services under normal terms or conditions with the one significant difference that the majority of employees are disabled people. Social enterprises are concerned with training, work experience and sheltered work. There may be a production of goods or services but this is not necessarily market-led and not intended to generate sufficient income to sustain a business that pays its workforce.

Policy Framework for Supported Employment

In 2000 the Policy Consortium for Supported Employment, which was established following discussions with Margaret Hodge, the then Minister for Equal Opportunities, produced a *Policy Framework for Supported Employment*. The report begins by acknowledging that the term 'supported employment' is currently used to cover a variety of different ways of working and clearly lays down its own definition. They define supported employment as a way of enabling people who need additional assistance to succeed in work with the following results:

- They are hired and paid by an employer
- They receive full employee entitlements
- The job meets the employees aspirations for employment
- The work meets the employer's entitlements
- The employer and employee receive just enough help from a support organisation to ensure success.

The report then looks in detail both at the current systems of supported employment in the UK and at the barriers that prevent disabled people from accessing it. It contains a section that draws parallels with supported employment provision in other countries and ends with putting forward various recommendations for change.

The report's conclusions are detailed and need to be read in full, but in essence it states that:

- Access to supported employment remains difficult for a large number of people who could benefit from it
- Funding is fragile and fragmented
- The benefit system can cause major problems for disabled people who want to enter employment
- There is little infrastructure to support the sector.

Possible national solutions include:
- More flexible use of funding
- The need for debate about more radical reform of the benefit system and other related subsidies
- The need for a broad-based approach to develop ways of measuring the quality of supported employment
- Identification of the key role of different stakeholders
- Ensuring that the strengths of supported employment are recognised by Personal Advisors.

At a local level it is seen as important that:
- The importance of supported employment is recognised
- Processes are developed that support the growth of supported employment
- All agencies work more closely together
- Effective welfare rights services are established.

Key messages for managers

The previous section gave a brief overview of recent policy initiatives. It showed how, although there is no over-riding statutory duty for organisations to provide programmes that support people into employment, there is a clear message from the government that organisations in all sectors should be looking at ways in which they can support more people with learning difficulties to gain meaningful work. This section looks at some of the key points that managers need to take into consideration.

Working together

It is clear that, if people with learning difficulties are to be supported into employment, different organisations will need to have ways of collaborating with each other. A key tool for this will be the new Learning Disability Partnership Boards referred to in the government White Paper, *Valuing People*. These Boards, which had to be in place by the end of October 2001, should have representatives from a range of organisations (Social Services, health, education, employment services, voluntary organisations). Their role will be to assess the need for provision, identify gaps and put in place long-term strategic plans. They will need to look specifically at provision that supports people with learning difficulties into employment. It is particularly important that post-school education should be seen as an active participant on these Boards. Questions managers may wish to ask are:

○ What are your organisation's strategies for working with other organisations?
○ Is your area of work represented on the newly forming Learning Disability Partnership Boards?
○ Are there clear lines of communication both to feed information down from the representative to managers and front line workers and also to feed information from front line workers up to the Board?

Liaising with the Connexions Service

If you are working with young people you should already have close links with the Connexions Service. Connexions Personal

Advisors will have a key role working with young people with learning difficulties on their personal action plans.

○ Is there a Connexions Service established in your area? If not who is currently providing advice for young people (this is likely to be the Specialist Careers Service)?
○ Do you have good links with this service?
○ Are workers in this service fully aware of the provision you offer so that they can discuss it with the young people they are advising?

Funding

Finding sufficient resources to fund quality provision is never easy. However, funding from one source can often be far more effective if it is used in collaboration with other funding sources. Even if one organisation is putting on excellent provision this will be less effective than it could be if it overlaps with provision put on by another organisation rather than complementing it. Different organisations need to work closely together to see how they might collaborate in order to produce a holistic offer.

○ Have you looked into the possibility of jointly-funded provision – either by merging funding or by creating holistic programmes that are funded by more than one agency?

Time for collaboration

Collaboration takes time. This time for liaising with other providers needs to be seen as an essential part of the programmes you offer.

Staff working in the area of supporting people into employment will need time:

- To find out about how other organisations work
- To find out about employment opportunities in their area
- To plan jointly with other organisations
- To liaise with other workers about individual student needs

○ Does your organisation recognise the importance of building liaison time into individual staff timetables?

Person-centred planning

Many of the policy initiatives referred to above emphasise the importance of planning that takes as its starting point the wishes and aspirations of individual people with learning difficulties. Historically, different agencies tend to have had established ways of delivering provision (for example Social Services day centres or college courses). Managers will need to work with staff to examine their traditional offer and see if it does respond appropriately to individual needs. This may require a substantial redesign of the structure and delivery of their provision and the development of more flexible programmes based on the principles of person-centred planning, which moves away from more traditional notions of course-based planning.

○ Is your organisation looking at its offer in the context of person-centred planning?
○ Is it examining other ways it could deliver provision so that it could respond more appropriately to individual needs and individual action plans?

References

The Disability Discrimination Act 1995 (as amended by the Special Educational Needs and Disability Act 2001) Draft Code of Practice Post-16, Disability Rights Commission

DfES (2002) *Providing Work Placements for Disabled Students: A good practice guide for further and higher education institutions*, Department for Education and Skills, Ref: DfES/0024/2002

DoH Publications (2001) *Valuing People: A new strategy for learning disability for the 21st century*, Department of Health Publications

Planning with People – Towards Person Centred Approaches:

Guidance for Partnership Boards

Guidance for Implementation Groups

Accessible Guide

Can be obtained free from:

Department of Health

Room 113, Wellington House

133–155 Waterloo Road

London SE1 8UG

These documents are also available on the Department of Health website at: www.doh.gov.uk

O'Bryan A, Simons K, Beyer S, Grove B (2000a) *A Framework for Supported Employment*, Joseph Rowntree Foundation

O'Bryan A, Simons K, Beyer S, Grove B (2000b) *Economic Security and Supported Employment*, National Development Team

Action plan

8

The chapters in this pack have given you a chance to reflect on some of the issues involved in developing provision that supports people with learning difficulties into employment. Although examples of transition to work provision were not easy to find, the Making the Jump project did find some practitioners who had been able to establish provision. The aim of this action plan is to draw together what is needed to establish a successful programme and to provide a checklist for those who want to develop provision of this kind.

Listening to learners

Listening to what learners themselves are saying is fundamental to developing any provision that supports them in their transition to work.

- ○ What do people with learning difficulties who you work with have to say about the issue of employment?
- ○ Do they want to work, and if so, what sort of work do they want to do?
- ○ Is there an independent self-advocacy organisation in your area you could work with that could support learners in having a say about their transition to work?
- ○ How can you ensure that the views and experiences of

people with learning difficulties inform the development of transition to work provision?

Involving parents and carers

Parents and carers are key players in supporting the transition to work. They may be very keen on the idea. They may also have understandable concerns.

- ○ How can you involve parents and carers and how can you keep them informed?
- ○ What support might you need to offer them?

Links with other organisations

The Making the Jump project has shown that programmes that aim to support people with learning difficulties into employment require close partnership between different agencies and organisations. Over and again case study examples have shown how such collaboration is crucial to success. Supporting the transition to employment for people with learning difficulties is a complex process and it is unlikely that it can be achieved by any one agency working in isolation. You will need to work with these agencies and organisations both at a strategic and a practical level. This might include liaison with those listed below.

The Local Learning and Skills Council

- ○ Are they aware of your work?
- ○ Who is your key contact there?
- ○ Is it clear that learners with disabilities or learning difficulties are a priority?
- ○ Are there ways the Council could support new developments?

The Learning Disability Partnership Board

- ○ Who is your representative on the Board?
- ○ Are there clear lines of communication between you and that representative?

The Connexions Service

- ○ Is there one already functioning in your area?
- ○ Who is your link person?
- ○ Are they aware of your provision?

The Employment Service

- ○ Who is your key contact?
- ○ Are they running provision that could link in with yours?

Social Services

○ Are they aware of what you are doing or hoping to do?
○ Are there ways you could work more closely together on supporting people into work?

Voluntary sector organisations

○ Are there voluntary sector organisations already working in ways that support people into work?
○ How might you link up with them?

The project has also shown that voluntary work can be an important first step for people with learning difficulties who wish to find paid work.

○ How do people find voluntary work in your area?
○ Have you had discussions with these organisations?

Links with employers

As well as forming partnerships with other organisations you will also need to have good relationships with local employers.

○ What are the main openings for employment in your area?
○ Are there any employers' groups who you could work with and raise the issue of work experience and paid employment for people with learning difficulties?
○ Do some of the partners you work with already have established links with employers' groups?

Benefits

It is very clear that the fear of being worse off when working than on benefits acts as a real deterrent to people with learning difficulties and their families. You will need to have close links with the Benefits Agency to ensure that there is someone who can give clear advice both in general and specific cases.

- ○ Do you have a named contact at the Benefits Agency?
- ○ Have you identified someone who understands the particular issues of benefits and people with learning difficulties who want to work?

Working with senior managers

Several of the case study sites emphasised the importance of having the support of senior managers when developing this kind of provision.

- ○ Have you worked closely with senior managers and shown them this pack?
- ○ Are they supportive of this work?
- ○ In particular do they recognise the need for staff to have time to liaise with other organisations and with employers if this work is to be successful?

Funding

The difficulty of funding this kind of provision was apparent throughout the project. Where funding had been found it was often fragile and short term.

- ○ Have you explored the possibilities of interagency funding to support this kind of work?
- ○ If your project is funded on a short-term basis have you got plans for incorporating it into the core programme when the specific grant runs out?

Curriculum

The curriculum framework for developing this kind of work needs to be flexible enough to respond to individual wishes and needs. It needs to do more than just work with people on employability skills as it also needs to ensure that those skills can be used in a real situation. Some key questions that need to be asked are listed below.

- ○ Is your curriculum flexible enough to allow for person-centred planning: that is plans that are based on the wishes and aspirations of individuals?
- ○ How can you ensure a balance between responding to individual agendas and enabling learners to have essential peer-group support?
- ○ How can you incorporate key and basic skills in a meaningful way into your curriculum?
- ○ Do the people you are working with have the opportunity to make informed choices about different kinds of work? For example by going on short work 'tasters'.
- ○ Is work experience incorporated into your curriculum offer in a way that makes it a relevant experience for people with learning difficulties?
- ○ How can you ensure that the notion of self-advocacy underpins your curriculum?

○ Is your curriculum respecting principles of equal opportunities (for example being accessible to the different needs of people of different races and different abilities)?

○ Has your curriculum framework ensured that your learners have ongoing support when they make the transition into employment?

Useful organisations

Learning and Skills Development Agency
Regent Arcade House
19–25 Argyll Street
London W1F 7LS
Tel: 020 7297 9000
Fax: 020 7297 9001
www.LSDA.org.uk

Mencap National Centre
123 Golden Lane
London EC1Y ORT
Tel: 020 7454 0454
Fax: 020 7608 3254
Minicom helpline (10am–4pm)
0808 8088181
www.mencap.org.uk

The National Development Team
Albion Wharf
Albion Street
Manchester M1 5LN
Tel: 0161 228 7055
Fax: 0161 228 7055
www.ndt.org.uk

National Institute of Adult Continuing Education
21 De Montfort Street
Leicester LE1 7GE
Tel: 0116 204 4200/1
Fax: 0116 204 4514
Minicom: 0116 255 6049
www.niace.org.uk

Norah Fry Research Centre
3 Priory Road
Bristol BS8 1TX
Tel: 0117 923 8137
Fax: 0117 946 6553
Minicom: 0117 928 8856
www.bris.ac.uk/Depts/NorahFry
www.plain-facts.org

Skill
The National Bureau for Students with Disabilities
Chapter House
18–20 Crucifix Lane
London SE1 2JW
Tel: 020 7450 0620
Fax: 020 7450 0650
Minicom: 0800 068 2422
Information line: 0800 328 5050
www.skill.org.uk

VIA
Values Into Action
Oxford House
Derbyshire Street
London E2 6HG
Tel: 020 7729 5436
Fax: 020 7729 7797
www.viauk.org

Welsh Centre for Learning Disabilities
Meridian Court
North Road
Cardiff CF14 3BG
Tel: 029 20691795
Fax: 029 20610812
www.uwcm.ac.uk/research/
research_groups

Appendix 1
Fieldwork visit sites for the Making the Jump – Transition to work project

Accrington and Rossendale College and Jigsaw Supported Employment

Amersham and Wycombe College and Buckinghamshire Agency for Supported Employment (BASE)

Blackburn College

Blakes and Link Employment Project Users Group, Hammersmith, London

Bolton Community Education Service and Bolton Employment Support Team (BEST)

Bournemouth & Poole College

Brent Mencap, London

CHANGE, London

CHANGE, Leeds

Croydon Continuing Education and Training Service (CETS)

Inca (Independent Neighbourhood Care Association), Manchester

Jigsaw Supported Employment, Clitheroe, Lancashire

Joseph Priestley College, Leeds

Loughborough Volunteer Centre

STATUS Employment, Croydon

Warrington Collegiate Institute

Pathway Employment Service at Harrow College

Appendix 2
Making the Jump –
Transition to work

Project findings sheet

Many people with learning difficulties fail to make the jump from attending further or adult education courses or Local Authority Social Services day services to paid employment. Making the Jump – Transition to work was a 2-year (2000–02) NIACE project, funded by the Department of Health. It set out to find examples of good practice of vocational courses or training where adults with learning difficulties are making the transition to employment.

Locating the provision

Examples of transition to work provision were rare and difficult to find. Vocational courses in further and adult education rarely include a transition process that supports the learner to progress onto employment. Where good transition to work provision does exist the numbers of people actually achieving employment are very low.

Working in partnership

All the examples of transition to work provision involved partnership working between different agencies. A link between education or training and some form of employment service, usually a supported employment agency, was essential for the success of transition to work provision.

Funding

Funding for transition to work provision was fragile. Pooling resources from several different sources was essential. Short-term funding can be valuable if it is used as pump-priming money. However, examples of provision funded in this way were vulnerable. If the provision is not incorporated into the core programme of courses on offer to people with learning difficulties, they tended to disappear when the grants ended.

Provision had been funded by:

- Learning and Skills Council
- New Deal for Disabled People
- Government Employment Services
- Local Authority Social Services Departments
- Lifelong Learning Partnership Businesses
- the European Social Fund.

Key factors for success

Several key factors for successful transition to work provision were identified. They include the need for the support of senior managers and the recognition that employment is a realistic goal for people with learning difficulties.

Benefits

The effect of earnings on benefits claimed by individuals was often perceived as a barrier. This influenced the level and type of employment sought by staff on behalf of people with learning difficulties. Having access to specialist advice and clear information about benefits was key to the success of transition to work provision.

Establishing provision

Transition to work provision was often the result of ad hoc arrangements. Provision that is developed as an integral part of educational opportunities on offer to people with learning difficulties was rare. In some areas, transition to work provision was being developed as part of an overall strategic plan of day services for people with learning difficulties. As such, it had some chance of becoming an established part of services on offer.

Learners' comments

Many people with learning difficulties valued the opportunity to train for work and progress onto employment.

'Give us a chance to show what we can do.'

'Never give up. Try and go for something you enjoy. People didn't think I could ever work.'

Policy context – *Valuing People*

In March 2001 the government issued the White Paper, *Valuing People: A new strategy for learning disability for the 21st century*. One of the key messages of the White Paper is the need to increase the number of people with learning difficulties accessing employment. It recognises that currently a number of different agencies are involved in supporting people with learning difficulties into employment and emphasises the necessity of far closer collaboration between Social Services and these other agencies.

Key features of effective transition to work provision

Researching the local employment situation is crucial. It can give transition to work provision a focus on specific skills that are in demand by employers. Learners will have an informed choice of actual employment opportunities that they can work towards. This makes the transition into employment much more of a reality. Supported employment organisations can be in a good position to do this research with their existing knowledge of the local situation and links with employers, businesses and other relevant organisations.

Working in partnership is a key feature of success. Effective transition to work provision will not develop unless agencies work together. The use of formal planning processes, such as Joint Investment Plans, can be very helpful with establishing links and developing partnership arrangements with other organisations.

Funding for sustainable transition to work provision is desperately needed. There is no set funding template for transition to work provision. Providers have to be creative and flexible in their approach to funding provision, drawing on various sources.

Parents and carers are an important part of any partnership involved in the development of effective provision. They need to be kept informed and involved in the planning of the transition process for their son or daughter.

Project fieldwork visits were made to further education colleges, adult and community education services, a volunteer centre, supported employment agencies, voluntary sector organisations run by and for people with learning difficulties and self-advocacy organisations. Managers, practitioners and people with learning difficulties who had or were making the transition to work, were interviewed about their experiences.

Further information on the staff and learners' pack based on the Making the Jump project can be obtained from the National Institute of Adult Continuing Education.

NIACE
21 De Montfort Street
Leicester LE1 7GE
Tel: 0116 204 4200/1
Fax: 0116 285 4514
Minicom: 0116 255 6049
Email: enquiries@niace.org.uk
Website: www.niace.org.uk